Decameron

Essays, Poetry and Art under Lockdown
5th April to 12th July 2020

The Bear Gates Traquair House, Innerleithen. Scotland.

Published by Beyond Lockdown Publications

First edition 2021

ISBN 9798746269478

This edition for Amazon print on demand (c) Lockdown Publications
2021

CONTRIBUTORS

Andrew Brown

Marie-Louise Brulatour Mills

Barbara Dickson

Jonathan Gibbs

Celine Hispiche

Dorothy Jackson

Roddy Martine

Jessie Ann Matthew

Mark McLeod

Catherine Maxwell Stuart

Mark Muller Stuart

Callum Stark

Pat Watson

Marie Weir

INTRODUCTION

Dear Friends,

AS a History of Art student at Edinburgh University, I read The Decameron by Giovanni Boccaccio in an English translation. It was written shortly after the Black Death of 1346 and tells various stories: witty, idyllic, tragic, erotic and comic by TEN friends secluded in quarantine in a villa in Fiesole overlooking plague-stricken Florence. During a period of two weeks with weekends off, each of the ten nominated a daily subject on subsequent days, and all of them recounted a poem, song, story or joke inspired by the theme. So over a period of TWO weeks, TEN people made ONE HUNDRED contributions in all.

I thought this would be an excellent plan for 10 friends and couples to follow by forming a group on WhatsApp and Zoom. However on reflection, I suspect our isolation might indeed be more like three months, so I propose over the next 100 or so days we each make one contribution every tenth day on the relevant theme so that by early July, when God willing, the plague may be over the worst, we will have 100 little masterpieces making a similar contribution to British culture and providing the same sort of insight into contemporary mores as Boccaccio did half a millennium ago. However, apart from prose and poetry, I propose we allow the occasional drawing, painting and video – but keep it brief. After all, according to "The Bard" brevity is the soul of wit.

As the instigator and moderator of this project, the first theme in light of our present situation is **HOME SWEET HOME**

ANDREW BROWN

TOPICS

1/ Home Sweet Home – Andrew Brown – 03/04/20

2/ Lemons – Marie Louise Brulatour-Mills - 13/04/20

3/ Serendipity – Roddy Martine - 23/04/20

4/ First Love – Barbara Dickson - 01/05/20

5/ Contrast – Callum Stark - 11/05/20

6/ Supernatural – Pat Watson - 21/05/20

7/ Act of Faith – Catherine Maxwell Stuart - 01/06/20

8/ Food for Thought – Dorothy Jackson - 13/06/20

9/ Transition – Mark Muller Stuart - 23/06/20

10/ New Horizons – Jonathan Gibbs and Jessie Ann Matthew – 04/07/20

Front cover: Alan Watson, "North Rona" 1992

Acrylic on canvas: 165cm x 165cm,

Copyright Pat Watson

In tune with the theme of lockdown and isolation, this painting by Alan Watson (1957-2019) explores what it might have felt like to be the last person on the remote Hebridean island of North Rona which is located in the Atlantic 45 miles from the north tip of Lewis. Uninhabited since 1844, Lewis shepherds still graze sheep there and tend to the island.

Alan never visited North Rona but was inspired to paint this picture by archive photographs of the deserted island. However the greatest influence on his work was the sad story of the most famous abandoned Hebridean island Saint Kilda which he had briefly visited on a school trip in the 1970s. He was determined to go back to Saint Kilda as it had completely captured his imagination. In 1984 supported by Scottish Arts Council grant, despite weeks of delay because of the weather, he finally made it over and was housed for a month with the nature conservancy warden helping to count and ring sea bird chicks. The drawing and sketches he made on that trip form the basis of a haunting series of paintings celebrating the uncompromising rocky landscape and the unique traditions of the islanders.

An exhibition of the paintings and drawings was mounted by the 369 Gallery at the Saltire society, Edinburgh in 1985.

HOME SWEET HOME

Andrew Brown

The Drowned Village.

I have always remembered my dear old university friend the late Derek Watson, composer and biographer of Wagner, telling me when we were students that the song Home Sweet Home and Wagner's Tristan and Isolde were written in the same year. I had never questioned his assertion until now, when I have discovered that my old friend was mistaken.

Tristan was written in the mid-1860s but Home Sweet Home was an aria from the deservedly forgotten opera The Maid of Milan, first performed in Convent Garden in 1823.

However, it is true that in the 1860s, during the American Civil War, Home Sweet Home became an unofficial anthem for home-sick union soldiers and appealed enormously to the sentimental imagination of late Victorian society on both sides of the Atlantic, into the middle of the 20th century. The chorus of it even becoming a magic mantra for Dorothy in The Wizard of Oz when she wanted to return home to Kansas and had to click her heels and repeat 'There is no place like home' three times, So that sent me off on a sentimental journey through all the many houses I have lived in since my first home as an infant in my Scottish grandparents' council house outside Edinburgh, where my very earliest memory is of crying over a cloth children's book illustrating farm animals, which I had left in the garden in the rain and the colours had run, my first lesson of the impermanence of things. As Buddha said, everything in life is pain, even pleasure, because you know it must end sometime.

As a slightly older child in the 1950s, I remember visiting my great aunt Agnes in the mining village of Bothwellhaugh near Hamilton, to which my Lithuanian grandparents had emigrated at the turn of the 19th century.

It was here that my father was born in a house in a street called Roman Road on the site of a real Roman road, adjacent to the Antonine Wall abandoned by the Romans less than 10 years after its construction, probably because of the rain and the midges I think, rather than the marauding Picts.

After the coal mine which supported the Lithuanian community closed, the village was abandoned in the 1960s and flooded under an artificial lake as the centrepiece of the Strathclyde Country Park, where the entire village lies beneath its obsidian surface.

This neatly brings me back to opera and Rimsky-Korsacov's

The Invisible City of Kitezh which, when under attack by the Tartars, sank beneath the waters of a lake only to reappear when safe to do so. Bothwellhaugh will never rise from the sooty water nor would its ruined back-to-back houses and boarded-up coop overlooked by a coal bing on which the children used to toboggan on old car tyres have the same poetic appeal as the frescoed churches and gilded onion domes of Kitezh.

But, my dear friends, though we now are submerged under this frightening virus like Kitezh, we too will one day soon emerge when it is safe to do so.

Roddy Martine

FOR writers, artists and musicians the supreme irony of self-quarantine in this challenging pandemic time is that in our being creative, we are always alone.

We are born alone. We die alone. In between is the chaos of humanity. There is nothing sad about this.

Creativity comes as a cynical distraction. Isolation from the herd is useful as it triggers the thought process.

Exposed on all sides, there is a genuine need among us to affect a formal distance from the ensuing chaos, if only to ensure our sanity. But this does not make us anti-social.

Quite the opposite when circumstances for self-indulgence occur (such as in this essay).

We love fun. We succumb to excess. Vanity seduces us all. We absorb the passions, the pleasures and the pain of others to produce the messages we seek in order to pursue our collective crafts.

Yet the chosen ones of Apollo must all have their Garbo moment. Ultimately, it is only through being on our own, wherever that may be for each and every one of us, that we find the time to conjure up the inspiration we so desperately seek.

As darkness falls, Home Sweet Home is our sanctuary. It is where we belong. It is where we shelter from, and attempt to interpret, the lives of others.

In such places, we surround ourselves with the collected keepsakes of our individual journeys; the secrets we cherish such as the favourite books, the photographs of departed loved ones, a broken toy, a primitive table from South East Asia, a souvenir of Switzerland, a porcelain figurine – the memorabilia of a life not quite almost unfulfilled.

These modest sparks of memory keep us engaged with the past. They travel with us in muted silence. The houses, the apartments we occupy change but such accumulated treasures of sentiment provide the continuity for which we all yearn.

They bring familiarity to the rooms in which we work, eat, sleep and dream, and in which we eventually hope to die.

When we are gone, they too will vanish. Or perhaps by some quirk of fate, they might reinvent themselves in some other Home Sweet Home and be similarly cherished by strangers in search of their own illusions.

Callum Stark

A platitude rings true in a pandemic.

I have a new found appreciation of that old turbo-cliché "Home is where the heart is."

On a recent state-approved walk through the evening streets of Edinburgh's South Side, I saw lone smokers tucked in doorways of almost every pub I passed: akin to the jolt of seeing an urban fox on an empty pavement. I fantasised that they were pub regulars returning like birds to a boarded-up nest, in a knee-jerk search for a shadow of the comfort and fellowship previously felt in these buildings.

This started me thinking about those corners of Edinburgh, of Scotland, and of the globe, which I think of as home.

I am lucky, where many aren't, to have a room of my own in which to shelter from the storm; however, it has taken a global pandemic to show me that home is not merely your address, but all of those places in which you feel most comfortable, where your tribe dwell, and – dare I say it – where your heart is.

I bring to mind the houses of friends in which I have spent innumerate nights in innumerate beds, and on the occasional floor; the murky clubs of the Cowgate – my nocturnal lodgings – whose darkened corners once seemed foreboding but now seem familiar; those restaurants where I would feel perfectly comfortable to lie down for a nap at the end of a long, sodden lunch. These, to me, are home.

So, for now, while I dwell in my place and my place alone, my bubble has not popped but merely shrunk, and as such, once this chapter departs, I will be ever more grateful for the space to roam, in every one of my home sweet homes.

Dorothy Jackson

WE are very lucky. We live in a house with ample rooms and a large garden. We also live in a rural area where it should be possible to self-distance without too much trouble. But in these trying times, we do all we can to reduce the danger.

Our house is a happy house. It was built in 1908 on the site of an orchard. Next door were glasshouses producing the produce that the Clyde Valley was famous for. Maybe after this is all over we will find a resurgence in cultivating our own produce.

We are only the second family to live in this house in its 112 years! The previous owners, a mother and daughter, lived across from us in a smaller house when the mother was 100 and both lived to a "ripe old age". Something to emulate – we hope.

They were a very forward thinking mother and daughter and moved with the times. Tolerant to the young families who moved in around them.

Tolerance is an emotive word but being non-judgemental is so important when we come under pressure.

Resilience is one of the most important qualities that young and old should possess. When we look back on this time, we will see wonderful examples of this.

We live right next door to the graveyard in Lanark and the ideal place to go for a walk whilst self-distancing. In this graveyard we have St Kentigern's Kirk.

This church is a scheduled ancient monument reputed to have been founded by St Kentigern shortly before his death in 603AD. There is also documentary evidence dating back to 1150AD and Pope Gregory IX took the church into its own protection in 1228.

All of this before the Black Death of 1347. It is reputed that the church was once attended by William Wallace and the more romantic of us believe the story that he married Marion Braidefute there.

Also, within sight of our house is Lanark Grammar School. It is one of the oldest schools in Scotland and received its charter from Pope Gregory VII in 1183.

The theme of this piece is "Home Sweet Home" and at this time we have never been more grateful for our sense of place and its surroundings.

Marie-Louise Brulatour Mills

I'm stuck in Rome
At another time it was home
The weather seems sunny
But I can't see it or the Easter bunny

Fridge is crowded with food and wine
Thanks to my children who took the time
Doing belly dancing to get back my line
and grateful to God to realign

To make greed and corruption a thing of the past
To reinstate principles to make them last
I am grateful for all that's been given and earned
God gave me life I can discern

Between the good and bad and people of worth
In spirit and care
Which we can now all share.

Mark Muller Stuart – Home Sweet Home

AT about 3am on 16th of February 1999, in Washington DC, James Rubin, Under-Secretary to the US State Department of the Clinton Administration, slowly turned to his side and stretched out his hand to pick up his bedside phone in a vain attempt to stop the muffled sound of sirens in his head. A few seconds later, he found himself sitting bolt upright staring intently into the darkness in a state of utter wakefulness.

Rubin's sudden early morning clarity was as a result of the transmission of a singularly explosive piece of intelligence. He had just been informed that the grey wolf had got its mountain goat.

It was the end of a remarkable five-month odyssey for one of the most wanted men in the world who was both simultaneously hated and loved by different nations and peoples alike. A man who had desperately scoured the earth in search of sanctuary and diplomatic intrigue on a global scale, at every corner.

A few minutes before Rubin picked up his phone, on the afternoon of 15th February 1999, a different set of sirens were heard along the dusty service road leading to Jomo Kenyatta International Airport on the outskirts of Nairobi, Kenya. These sirens belonged to two Kenyan security jeeps hurtling towards the airport in the searing afternoon heat of an African sun.

Both jeeps were packed with soldiers armed with automatic rifles. In between the jeeps were two vehicles – one black car with "Police" inscribed on its side, and another car, also black, but this time with diplomatic plates.

The sirens cut though the late afternoon air like an executioner's axe as the cars sped unforgivingly past the forgotten shanty districts that line the route to Nairobi Airport.

All around, people momentarily turned their heads towards the ensuing noise only to return their attention back to the business of their day, oblivious to the world drama unfolding before them. People who would remain silent but nameless witnesses to the abduction of the hopes of another invisible people, who lived in an ancient land thousands of miles away from Africa.

In fact, the people of Nairobi's shanty districts were used to the endless processions of official vehicles, diplomatic plated cars, and jeeps on security details whose purpose was to protect the hides of Africa's rich and powerful, as they tore remorselessly each day through the pot-holed streets of their ramshackle homesteads.

Such processions had become almost invisible to them. Even their children had developed a sixth sense about the impending arrival of Africa's metallic bullets like swarms of Mosquitoes evading a death clap. But today's procession was different. There was something different about the way these particular security vehicles moved.

It wasn't just the high speed. It was the expert manner with which they rounded the corner. It was the way they effortlessly read the potholed terrain in front of them. And it was the sense that nothing, no pothole, bus, cart, human or beast, was going to stop those vehicles from reaching their destination.

And there was something else too – something odd about the man sitting in the back of the black police car and something different about the officials who surrounded him. These security officials stared menacingly out towards the huddled masses on the broken footpaths as if to forestall some imaginary military ambush. Yet the stares were not ones of protective concern for their human cargo but of something else.

The man in the back of the car didn't look like a diplomat or visiting dignitary. Neither was he black nor white but rather a dirty colour and unshaven. Yet, nor did he look as if he was under arrest either. There were no signs of handcuffs.

And why should the police be taking a suspect towards the airport anyway when Nairobi Detention Centre was in the opposite direction?

No, the oddest thing about the man in the black police car was the way he was sitting. He sat as if he was frozen – frozen in posture, frozen in his stare and frozen in time.

This eerie disposition was in complete contrast to the people in the diplomatic car that followed the frozen man in the black police car. Ordinarily onlookers from the airport shanty districts paid little attention to the superior demeanour of the immaculate occupants of such diplomatic cars. Just as those seated within such cars paid little attention to the miserable world passing before them, save, that is, for the odd outward imperial gaze without so much as a flicker of human recognition.

But the occupants of the diplomatic car were noticeably different both in deportment and demeanour. There was nothing remotely regal or imperial about the occupants of this car.

The two female occupants in the back of the diplomatic car appeared besides themselves with anxiety. Both women perched forward frantically pointing in the direction of the black police car ahead. They were screaming. Their faces, which were neither black nor white but olive brown like the man in the back of the other police car, constantly turned and darted from window to window.

Unlike the officials in the first car, these faces stared out of the windows in wild-eyed desperation, as if caught in a fatal vortex not of their making, searching out in forlorn hope for a would-be super-hero who could rescue them from an unknown plight.

In the front of this car sat a well-dressed man who seemed more accustomed to the superior surroundings of the car. A diplomat of sorts – of that there could be no doubt.

But he too looked agitated. Perhaps more pensive than agitated.

It was difficult to know whether the women were screaming at him or at the other car. It seemed like both. But in any event, he seemed more concerned with whoever he was talking to on the phone.

He seemed to be in a desperate search for instructions. Yet he also had a fatal air of resignation about him – the air of resignation of a person who knew that whatever the instructions he received his fate had already been sealed, like a character out of a Greek tragedy.

Within a few seconds this strange cavalcade, with its portentous sirens and strange mixture of occupants, had passed by as quickly as it had come into view, as the Shanty District of Nairobi Airport returned once more to its monotonous, poverty-stricken normality.

A few minutes later a small executive Falcon jet tore down the runway of Nairobi Airport to the exalted high five hand clapping of its adrenalin-fuelled occupants. All, that is, except for one passenger who found himself, handcuffed, blindfolded and frozen in terror. "Let there be no torture," he intoned.

Back on the runway, the security vehicles that had surrounded the small jet air-craft just moments before began to disappear almost as quickly as they had appeared, including one carrying a variety of Caucasian security officials who immediately peeled away from their Kenyan counterparts as soon as the aircraft took off.

Within a minute or two, all of the officials and vehicles that surrounded the aircraft had unceremoniously vanished. While outside, by the perimeter fence near the V.I.P. reception area of the airport, two Kurdish women screamed into a mobile phone and began to wail in complete contortion as the black car with diplomatic plates that had transported them to Nairobi Airport sped off leaving them to an uncertain fate.

Over the next few months, no-one would think to ask the people of the Shanty districts of Nairobi what some of them might have seen that day. Not one official, journalist or lawyer ever made the laborious trek out to the rat-infested suburbs to re-cord what these residents may have witnessed along the Airport road in the late after-noon of 15th of February 1999.

No newspaper nor television station ever carried their stories. No court ever came to rely upon their testimonies. These forgotten people with their undocumented obser-vations remained, as ever, invisible to all concerned.

Yet anyone who did see that odd cavalcade of cars pass through Nairobi that day would not have been in the slightest doubt as to what they had just witnessed if, that is, like Nairobi's diplomatic community and band of motley foreign correspondents, they had access to the world's press and media the next day.

For they would have realised that what they had just inadvertently witnessed was one the of the world's first extraordinary renditions by a group of Western States.

A rendition of not only one of the most wanted men in the world but also of his, and a forgotten people's, search for recognition and justice. A rendition of such consequence for a group of nations and peoples alike, that its impact continues to cause political reverberations around the world, even to this day.

A rendition of Abdullah Ocalan - rebel leader of the Kurdistan Workers Party, the PKK – who was loathed, feared and revered in equal measure by the peoples of a region who now variously held their breath in collective anticipation, celebration and anguish.

As the Falcon exited Kenyan air space for the open unregulated skies - and the hopes of a people were once again cruelly dashed and betrayed by an unholy international alliance – its drugged, handcuffed and blindfolded human cargo was heard to finally mutter, "Where are they taking me?"

Terror once more took hold of his dislocated body and disorientated mind as he heard the voice of a Turkish commando whisper quietly into his ear,"Now don't you worry – all will be alright – for you're going 'home sweet home,' and with that he fell into a deep, thoughtful and melancholic sleep.

Mark with Sydney Kentridge QC before opening the case of Oculan v Turkey before the Grand Chamber of the European Court of Human Rights in Strasbourg

on 9th July 2004

Marie Weir

A letter from the farm at Kilness during the First World War

My dearest,

I write to you with news of Kilness as I feel that I must do something routinely as you are so starved of information being so far from home.

The farm goes well despite the young men who feel that they must do their bit for their country — that just leaves the men over 40 to keep all in running order. Thankfully, we are not really an arable farm so the tending of the beasts and the sheep are not so bad with the help of the young boys who are not old enough to take the King's Shilling — the lambing starts in January so now the animals are quite big and are now fully weaned.

This is a blessing as we have not lost many due to the weather conditions which have remained quite unseasonal. I do hope that wherever you are that you are keeping dry and warm. Thankfully the weather is starting to heat up just in time for the calving season, so hopefully all will go well in preparation for your return.

I am busy knitting socks, gloves and balaclavas for the Red Cross to pass on to you brave soldiers — the young girls are also knitting whenever time permits but I detect a current of displeasure that they are unable to help with the war effort which is increased by the call of HM Factory Gretna for young girls to contribute to the war effort — the War Factory has been built to include housing, food canteens, and leisure opportunities as well as paid work units which are very attractive to the young unmarried local girls who seek independence both financially and to give them a sense of adventure living away from home. Kilness can spare these young girls as I can easily take over their duties of milking and feeding the hens although home baking may be in a shorter supply due to lack of time!

It is with great sadness that I write of the two young farmworkers who signed up to a Pals unit after the requisition of all farm horses for the frontier — Ian and Dougie McMillan felt that they were needed much more at the front than farming at Kilness and they gave their lives valiantly at the Battle of The Somme. I can only hope that they will be remembered in perpetuity for their courage in the years following this global conflict.

I must end now and on a positive note and hope that all is well with you. You must not worry about the farm at Kinloss as we are all doing fine and we look forward to welcoming you back home with open arms — all in the near future, of course.

MW: Good afternoon unfortunately due to my non-IT skills I was unable to join in the chat of Decameron last night. Anyway, I would have added that my letter to a soldier of the Great War was fiction based on some facts. Therefore, on Tuesday last I ventured down to the WW1 memorial in Holywood Churchyard to rediscover the names of the 2 men who gave their lives – both by the name of Craig but there was no mention of their dates or where they died. Of the 26 from the parish who died the memorial only gave their names, regiment and where they resided. Imagine my surprise when at the very bottom of the list was another from Kilness. On returning home I googled their names but to little success – however, I did find out that Kilness had 3 male farm workers and one female servant. I wonder if she was the ghost that I had seen on two occasions prior to the death of my mother and husband. I have never seen her since.

The three soldiers of Kilness who never returned from the Great War are - according to their memorial – Ernest Leslie Craig of Kilness who was in The Royal Scottish; George Lyell Craig who joined the K.O.S.B. and William McLeod who was in the Scottish Rifles. No birthdates or place and time of death are given so speculation must question the relationship between the 2 Craigs. I would love to know the history of these men who gave their lives for us and live in perpetuity on the WW1 memorial in Holywood Churchyard.

PW: There are three Craigs all from Kilness, a sad story here perhaps.

MW: Thank you as my googling just gave English census rather than 1911 Scottish census which should/may have mentioned them. Please let me know what/ if anything you find x

PW: Re Craig family, Scotland Monumental Inscriptions, Ernest Leslie Craig, Death year 1917 Place Hollywood, Dumfriesshire, Inscription: Erected to the Memory of Joseph Craig, joiner, Kilness, died 20th June 1915 aged 63 years Also of his sons: James Gordans, killed in action at Arras 11th April 1917 aged 20 years George Lyell, KOSB, killed in action at Armentieres 6th June 1918 aged 25 years Ernest Leslie, R Scots, killed in action at Arras 11th April 1917 Henry, ex KOSB, died at Dalkeith 15th January 1919 aged 41 years. Also Margaret Craig, wife of the above, who died at West Crosslets 27th December 1933 aged 75 years (c) Dumfries and Galloway Family History Society. From Find My Past website. Poor Margaret, so sorry to find this X

MW: So sad but they died for us and their country – they should never be forgotten.

Interesting that there are more WW1 deaths than those suggested on war memorial … or have I misinterpreted it.

PW; No it was a real muck up then as well as now. Who was and is the point?

MW: Just looked at war memorial again, I had not noticed that there was mention of three Craigs – how awful for the mother to lose her three sons.

AB: Good Friday. We are planning a zoom conference of our Decameron participants organised by Callum Stark at 6pm when Marie-Louise, technology willing from the roof of the palazzo Pozzi in Rome, will choose the theme for the next 10 days

DJ: Sounds good. Not sure if I can cope with this! I do have zoom. I'll try. ❤

AB: This sounds like the work of the Devil but I'm always willing to try anything once.

Jonathan Gibbs

CLOSE-UP: A home is safely enclosed by the heart, held within its curving sides.   An arrow is balanced at the apex of the heart. A line from the tip circles the form whilst pointing away from its centre.

Catherine Maxwell Stuart

HOME has not always been sweet to me. Having grown up in a house that has seen generations of my family live here for over half a millennium there were times when I couldn't wait to get away. As a teenager I craved the city, anonymity and freedom from the overbearing history of the place. The endless portraits of ancestors staring down, slightly disapprovingly, I always thought, of my youthful exploits.

It was so refreshing when I remember discovering the letters of Lady Louisa Stuart born in the 1770s and brought up at Traquair.

In an early letter, she complained that she wished Traquair could be transported to Richmond so she could enjoy a more exciting social life. I knew exactly how she felt.

In fact, Louisa herself was transported to the South when her mother died. It was felt inappropriate that she live alone with her father so she was sent to live with relatives.

There are some touching and hilarious letters to her father whom she was evidently very close to, and Traquair which she missed.

On one occasion, she reminded him where to find his winter underclothes in the bottom drawer of a chest and in another, in great excitement, she exhorts her father to be properly dressed for the visit of George IV to Edinburgh.

She tells him to get a new wig and to ensure that it is "life hair and not the hair of a hanged man."

Many years later she returned to Traquair and lived with her brother, both unmarried, to the remarkable age of 99 years and 5 months. We have a photograph of her looking like an aged Queen Victoria. She clearly loved her home deeply and with her brother they were devoted to improving the estate, setting up the new St Ronans artesian well in Innerleithen and supporting the new railway.

She is also our grey lady who is seen walking in the grounds on summers' afternoons. A local farm worker having seen her apparition float through a gate into the woods checked with the granddaughter of a dressmaker of Lady Louisa and recognised from a swatch of material that it matched the dress he had seen the lady wearing on that day.

Of course, I have found my own way back to Traquair and have become intrinsically connected with this place that is part of me. We live with each other supporting each other through the years, although unlike Louisa I am grateful that I do so with a family. I am often asked about the ghosts here and I always reply that there have been no murders or violence at Traquair so there are no restless spirits to haunt us.

RM to CMS: I love the idea of ghosts returning to watch over places they lived in in their lives. I am certain they do. X.

CS: Andrew and I were thinking that it would be interesting to do a sort of virtual salon at the end of every ten days or so, via Zoom (it's not as complicated as you might think). So, the first one would be in three days or so. What does everyone think?

Traquair House – Innerleithen.

Mark McLeod

THE first and maybe only "home" in my life which evokes the positive & loving feelings associated with Andrew's first theme is not the one I and my siblings grew up in nor the one I live in now. Rather, they are firmly routed in and around our paternal grandparents' house where we used to have occasional sleepovers when we were all much younger.

I would have been around 10 years old or so, my sister 8, and my wee brother 6, and we used to look forward so much to the treat of a night at granny and grandpa's. Perhaps it was because we had a 6th sense as kids that things weren't great at home in our parents' marriage (soon after these sleepovers, divorce came) that we jumped with joy to spend time in a place where the environment was – nothing – other – thanfull – of unconditional love and affection.

The house was a small 2 bedroom council house in West Lothian which my grandparents lived in for over 40 years before they both died.

The routine was always the same – small snacks as we chatted, laughed and watched Sat night TV as a group with the coal fire raging (the opening credits of "Juliet Bravo" come to mind!)

When it came to bedtime, my younger brother would change into his PJ's in the living room before then heading upstairs to one of the 2 bedrooms – a bedroom with 2 single beds. He climbed into what was my grandpa's single bed (we never wondered why our grandparents slept in 2 single beds).

That was him for the night but he told me recently that he hated having to be the first one leaving the rest of us downstairs. About 30 minutes later or so, my sister got changed for bed in the living room. Up she then went to the other single bed normally slept in by my granny. My sister recalls the bed being made "hospital style" and so tight that it took all her strength to manage to open enough of an opening between the sheets to manage to get in to them.

My granny who always felt the cold more than anyone, used to have old fashioned flannelette sheets AND a hot water blanket which was always switched on. Maybe it's for this reason that my sister, to this day, also seems super sensitive to the cold herself.

My sister doesn't remember falling asleep but remembers waking up to our little granny sharing the bed with her fast asleep. As the "big boy", I was allowed to stay up half an hour later and it felt special to be sitting there with my 2 grandparents on a Sat night, just the three of us.

I was treated to a mug of hot Bovril and more snacks before I too then got into my pyjamas. I then headed upstairs to the 2nd small bedroom and into the only double bed in the house.

I don't remember falling asleep but I do remember waking up on the Sunday morning to find my grandfather sleeping beside me, him in his PJ's with handkerchief in the pocket.

Morning routine was always the same – granny was up early and could be heard downstairs in her kitchenette making porridge. Like 2 kings upstairs, she would come up and serve both my grandad and me our bowls in bed.

Sitting up in bed beside him as we both ate our breakfast felt magical and special.

This was another world from "back home." After the trays were taken away, another smaller tray appeared and my grandad plugged in an old fashioned electric razor to have a dry shave in bed catching his whiskers on the small tray!

I look back now and realise how unique and special these loving nights and mornings were.

CMS to MM: Perfect! I can smell the Bovril.

DJ: A very loving piece

AB: Lovely now I understand why the original Decameron was such a treasure of seemingly inconsequential but unique details to future historians, x

BD: Mark, your tale of your kind and loving grandparents' unconditional love is very moving. Thank you. X

MMS: Thank you Mark your Decameron made me suddenly recall the crisp, clean and brilliant white goose feathered Black Forest duvet in which I was wrapped by my German grandmother at Xmas time in the small spa town of Bad Durrheim surrounded in snow near Lake Constance as the white candles continued to flicker on the tree in the old drawing room downstairs where my grandfather would drink schnapps after Xmas eve and avoid trying to talk to his brother-in-law, Uncle Willie, about the war, who emerged from a Russian POW camp after 8 years with the most extraordinary glint in his eye and zest for life as to put Andrew to shame – and also from the travails of Stalingrad where 3 of my Grandmother's brothers died in the frozen waste.

DJ: Billy's grandmother and Aunt Marta also lived on Lake Constance in Bergenz. His aunt worked in a cotton mill and lived there until she died about 2010. He had many happy holidays there apart from him ending up in hospital with pneumonia!

LEMONS

DJ: Happy Easter to you all!

BD: Yes, Happy Easter. Alleluia, alleluia!

CMS: Happy Easter to all! Enjoying not having to hide 5,000 eggs now that the Traquair Easter egg hunt has been cancelled due to COVID. All went to the hospital and local community hubs.

DJ:: Glad the eggs got good homes Catherine. A lovely use of them. 🐣🌈🌷

RM: Happy Easter to all.xxx

Marie-Louise Brulatour Mills

Sun warming my back
in black and hat
St Peters in distance
With dominating insistence
lemons maturing
Honeysuckle and jasmine reassuring
The fragrance of lemons squeeze them a lot
My children matured and they all forgot
What a squeeze can mean
to hold and feel an old lemon seen
Is in that field of love and learning
or caring for all discerning
a squeeze of the zest
is a lesson we can do best.

PW: Marie Louise, your thoughtful poem stays with me, thank you for sharing x

Dorothy Jackson

AS a child, my experience of lemons was probably first associated with breaded fish. My mother also used to make home-made lemonade which I adored. It was tart but also sweet. When I look at the list of ingredients, it looks most unusual: citric acid, Epsom salts, lemons and sugar!

To a child these were strange ingredients indeed. In the early 1960s, my mother went on a slimming diet and introduced a magical ingredient called PLJ into her diet regime. This was meant to "burn" the fat away. The advertisement at the time suggested that taking lemon juice at daybreak was a daily rule for figure and complexion care!

She drank this with water in the morning. It was many years until I realised the PLJ stood for pure lemon juice. I also remember those little Jif lemons which were kept in the fridge for a long time. As a child I loved the fact that they were shaped like a lemon.

Now my association with lemons is more likely to be connected with gin! I also associate lemon with Limone sul Garda in the Lombardy region of Italy. This region has risen in prominence during the pandemic as one of the first two areas in Italy to have Covid 19. The other being the Veneto region. I revisited Limone last year for a short holiday and found it to be as charming as it have been almost 20 years before.

In September 1786, Goethe passed the village by boat and wrote the following:"We passed Limone, the mountain gardens of which, laid out terrace-fashion, and planted with citron-trees, have a neat and rich appearance. The whole garden consists of rows of square white pillars placed at some distance from each other, and rising up the mountain in steps. On these pillars strong beams are laid, that the trees planted between them may be sheltered in winter. The view of these pleasant objects was favoured by a slow passage and we had already passed Malcesine when the wind suddenly changed, took the direction usual in the day-time, and blew towards the north."

On alighting from the ferry from Riva del Garda, one of the first views I had was of shops selling lemons and lemon related gifts.

My plan was to visit Italy again this year but the trip has been cancelled and I real-ise that I will need to be patient.

There's always gin and tonic with lemon and ice to keep my taste buds suitably quenched and what about Limoncello from the Sorento area?
Now there's a thought!

r SORRENTO

Pat Watson

I was musing about what lemon means to me over a cup of tea this morning.

My memory of lemon is entwined with happy memories of family and friends.

From my childhood baking a lemon meringue pie with my brother for Sunday tea, helping my father make a batch of lemonade on warm summer days, high tea at Granny's, ham, tomato and buttered bread or scrambled eggs followed by scones and pancakes from her tiered cake stand with home made lemon curd or jam, only then cake.

Home cooked breaded Pittenweem haddock and chips on a Saturday night with Alan and the children.

Opening the bar with a G&T of an evening while sharing our experiences of the day while preparing dinner.

The relaxed atmosphere and the gentle murmur of chatter and bird song seated on the rustic balcony under the canopy of tall trees at Pillars of Hercules Organic Farm Shop & Cafe near Falkland.

Enjoying their lemon cake with coffee or tea. Sharing stories, putting the world to rights, shared laughs over a jug of Pimms with our friends in their beautiful garden in Kent.

I wonder what my memory of lemon from today might be? Possibly cleaning lime scale from taps?

St Kilda by Alan Watson 1984 (for his mother)

Roddy Martine

LEMONS? A yellow citric fruit with a bitter taste best enjoyed with gin and tonic. Lemonade? No, I thought. Citron Presse, a sharp refreshing drink which I discovered while on a French language course in the summer heat of the Riviera.

I was all of fifteen and It was years before I tumbled into the routine of claret and scotch (not mixed together, mind you), and vodka, as I was yet to discover, is a killer.

Citron Presse – such memories.

I was billeted on the widowed Madam Epron on the second floor of a villa over-looking the waterfront in Menton. Two German brothers around my own age occupied the second bedroom – Gerald and Peter Warbergen.

Gerald, the eldest, svelt and loud, displayed all the brutish charm of a trainee Hitler youth. His younger brother Peter, sweet with saucer blue eyes, was an innocent in thrall to his brother's ruthless Prussian self-confidence.

The apartment was small and sparsely furnished with crucifixes hanging on the walls and a framed black and white photograph of General de Gaulle meeting the Pope in the hallway. I slept in Madam's abandoned and squeaky marital bed with its frayed patchwork quilt and I initially wondered where she herself slept until one night, after midnight, I strayed into the bathroom and found her curled up in a rug in the bath tub. No wonder she encouraged us to shower on the beach.

It only occurred to me then that despite her chique and impeccable dress sense, the rent Madam Epron was paid for board and lodging was probably her only source of income.

There were twenty of us on the French language course – seven girls and thirteen boys. We were a cosmopolitan mix of American, German, British and Scandinavian. There was Frank, coincidentally from Innerleithen in Scotland; Belinda from Stockholm, Karl, who told us his father owned most of Hawaii, and the Mayor of Casterbridge's daughter Lily.

By any standards, Lily was a Pre-Raphaelite beauty. Medium height and sweet, her ice green eyes were set in peach perfect skin. She was one of those redheads who preferred to be acknowledged as a strawberry blonde.

Of course, so far as she was concerned the rest of us were far too young, especially Gerald who saw her as a macho challenge. Perhaps it was inevitable she should take up with a muscly Algerian boy with a motor scooter whom she met on the beach.

We all knew what was going on. None of us resented her having fun. Some of us were even envious and we covered for her when she turned up late for the daily roll call.

Oh, but what a summer we had! Classes every week day morning. Blissful afternoons spent diving into the sea from offshore pedalos.

Most Côte d'Azure beaches are pebbly and, in those days more than a trifle insanitary. As you swam to your raft fifty or so yards from the shore, It was not unusual to encounter floating fried eggs and toilet rolls. A swarm of jelly fish more often than not was nothing more than a school of discarded condoms.

On one occasion we were taken to a ruined church to hear the soprano Elizabeth Schwarzkopf sing Romanian folk songs under a vast and starlit sky. The ballet dancer Rudolf Nureyev, recently absconded from Russia, was sitting with his friend Eric Bruhn in the row in front of us and I asked him for his autograph. I mentioned this to him over twenty years later when I interviewed him in Paris. "Ah, but you were a little boy then. You are a big boy now," he laughed.

And so I was, but it was in Menton that I was first introduced to lieder under the Milky Way and where I first came across those little tubs of fruit yoghurt, then unobtainable in the UK. More to the point, it was in Menton that I acquired a taste for Citron Presse, the only drink other than coca-cola available if you were under age which, though we all tried hard to deny it, we obviously were.

Every evening before returning to our lodgings for supper, our little group would gather together to compare sun-tans on the Promenade du Soleil and drink copious non-alcoholic quantities of the lemon concoction with a spoonful of sugar.

Free from parental control, we were all so young and free and naive and every one of us felt so very, very grown up drinking... lemon juice, water and sugar? Perhaps it was the very name – Citron Presse – that suggested some forbidden adult pleasure, some crashed car of desire.

Lily, meanwhile, wanted nothing to do with us. Although Gerald pressed his suit relentlessly, sitting as close to her as possible in the schoolroom and being ignored. When midday arrived, she would rush to the door and be glimpsed moments later on the pillion seat of the Algerian's scooter.

She made it abundantly clear that she was simply not interested in making friends with us. While the other girls bonded and bitched about her, it was patently obvious they were jealous. I sometimes wondered if our adult group leader or for that matter, her landlady, had any inkling of what was going on.

Meantime, I had Gerald to put up with.

For our supper every Thursday evening, Madam Epron would provide Gerald, Peter and I with, in her own words, a "vrai regal." This took the form of a raw steak. Unaccustomed to eating uncooked meat, I felt sick but with the good manners of my upbringing, managed to overcome my nausea.

On the second week, I was seated beside Gerald when he dropped his fork onto the floor. I instinctively leant over to retrieve it and when I sat up again, I found he had slid his grisly untouched raw steak onto my plate. In that instance Madam returned from the kitchen and seeing my plate supposedly untouched, exclaimed, "Tu n'aime pas ma cuisine?" She looked so upset.

With a weak smile, I cut it up and swallowed. How I hated Gerald.

All good things must come to an end and on the night before we were scheduled to return home, there was a barbecue at the tennis club. Saying goodbye to friends, most of whom you know you will never see again, is bound to be emotional.

Gerald had somehow acquired a couple of bottles of vodka and although none of us realised it at the time, Citron Presse took on a life of its own. The mood grew merry and uninhibited, and suddenly there was Lily, no doubt realising that for appearances sake she needed to put in an appearance for our tutors. More surprising still, she was accompanied by the Algerian boy, dark and unexpectedly menacing.

Now whether it was the alcohol or the realisation that her holiday romance was coming to an end, but Lily suddenly flung her arms around Gerald and kissed him passionately on the lips.

It was then I saw the knife. A quick slash and a four inch cut of blood appeared on Lily's lovely face. The next thing I knew was that Gerald had buckled up with a groan. While Frank and Karl and I feebly attempted to restrain the Algerian boy, he broke away from us and escaped on his scooter.

Remember that this was in an age before mobile phones. After an interminable wait, the gendarmerie arrived with an ambulance and Lily and Gerald, accompanied by Peter, were taken to the nearest hospital. Although we were afterwards reassured that both had recovered, the latter was presumably scarred for life. I never saw them again.

former

I did, however, keep in touch with Frank and Belinda and, as it turned out, Karl's father really did own half of Hawaii.

That night in Menton we all came of age. Years later I read that Gerald had been elected to the Bundestag. On a personal note, I have only since crushed and drunk the juice of a lemon to combat a winter cold.

Marie Weir

I remember once reading that children are categorised by which position they are born into a family.

As one of eight children born to a Catholic family it is easy to categorise the first five children – boy – adored by all relatives and much made of with great expectations; the second child – girl – lives in her elder brother's shadow and is seen only as female; the third – boy – is regarded as the family joker and much also made of; four and five – girls very close together in birth – are treated as twins with number four being the dominant.

I was born number two and was seen as the 'home-maker' and 'little mother' - a role I didn't appreciate but it was easier to acquiesce than refute, although secretly there was no way I was going to fulfil that role!

For example when I had just started secondary 2 – and my father, returned from working in Russia, decided to move out of the city to become self-employed in rural Scotland – my mother said that after school I was to go to 'Do School' and then help her run a Bed and Breakfast business. I had no idea what 'Do School' was but I agreed for a quiet life but no way was I doing what another wanted me to do!

I remember that as 'the home-maker' I was cooking Saturday lunch for the whole family by the time I was in P4/5 – at first helping my mother then taking over making Shepherd's Pie/American Bean Pie followed by custard while she regarded Saturday as her day off by having a lie in, lunch and dishes done by myself, each Saturday afternoon spent at the hairdresser's and evening at 'Scottish Country Dance Classes' which, in hindsight, was probably a misnomer for an evening spent at the Parkhead bingo with her sister.

I was in Secondary 2 when we moved to an idyllic seaside country village and Saturday afternoons were spent 'home-making' by baking – and my piece de resistance?

Lemon Meringue Pie which my father was especially fond of. I continued in the 'home-maker' role until I escaped back to the city and Edinburgh University to study History and English at the end of Secondary 6 – I have never made a Lemon Meringue Pie since!

What I really look forward to doing after this lockdown is to go out for tea in the afternoon – a smoky black loose leaf like Lapsang or Tarry Souchong or Russian Caravan. Failing that, a nice cup of Earl Grey – with lemon, of course – and a slice of cake preferably lemon drizzle!

Catherine Maxwell Stuart

THERE is something so exquisite and delicious about a perfect lemon tart that it is my all time favourite dessert.

The secret is to master the most indulgent of all recipes so the lemon is at its most intense with just the right amount of tartness and a background of a creamy richness that it can only be eaten in the smallest amounts with a generous serving of double cream.

It was the first dinner party dessert that I ever made that impressed. Back in the eighties, when the River Cafe cook book first came out and we were all frantically trying to make our own pasta with disastrous results, I discovered the lemon tart.

This recipe contains 15 eggs, the juice and zest of 7 lemons and enormous quantities of butter. It

takes time and energy to make: zesting, squeezing, whipping but the result is truly worthwhile.

I made one last night. Unbelievably none of my family likes a lemon tart so I am going to have to freeze it and wait for our post lockdown party to share!

BD: This sounds yummy! Oh, my taste buds are tingling!!!

AB: I'd happily demolish one for you now Catherine x

Callum Stark

Luck be a Lemon

I recently read that love of bitter tastes is one common in psychopaths. I would put forward that a penchant for the sour things in life is, too, indicative of a subversive personality and a culinary imbalance. From infancy, sucking on lemons has been one of my peculiar pleasures

As with many addictions, it's a satisfaction that is double edged: the balance of enjoyment and repulsion so exact as to keep me coming back for yet another (citric) hit. I've even been known to fish the lemon wedges out of companion's cocktail glasses, for a squeeze of gin addled sourness.

But lemons hold memories of a different sort for me also, memories of a school trip – aged fifteen or so – to the Amalfi Coast. I, with three friends found a limoncello shop, while wandering the back streets of Portofino, or was it Sorrento?

After sufficient nudging (from me), a friend, fluent in Italian, purchased a bottle of limoncello from the evidently unscrupulous shop keeper, who also stocked a wide range of citrus filled phalluses in a variety of shapes, and indeed, sizes. Why, I can't remember, but we left that shop with the most miniscule bottle, no bigger than a few inches tall.

That evening the four of us gathered as my friend proceeded to turn her dorm into the world's least jolly pub. It all felt so pointlessly sordid as she poured to each their allotted few millimetres, A few millimetres that my friend was subsequently to spill by the pool, which we thought was a fittingly anticlimactic end to this pathetic act of rebellion.

However, this proved to be merely the prologue to the high melodrama to come, as the pupils of another school staying in the camp were busted with their own more substantial supply of limoncello.

Dorms were raided. Bottles were hidden. They falsely accused members of our school as the dealers of the illicit substance and with bitter-sweet irony, it was not me, nor any of my friends indicted, but two entirely innocent girls in my year. For reasons of space and decorum I am unable to outline the subsequent events, except to say that when I think of lemons, I think of luck.

Mark Muller Stuart

The Sweeter Side of Bitter lemons

AS soon as the word 'Lemons' appeared on Decameron, my mind's eye inevitably travelled back to my house and time in Kyrenia (Girne to the Turkish Cypriots) with its crescent harbour and collection of white and beige houses and seaside restaurants nestling alongside an imposing Venetian fort, flanked by the absurdly dramatic 12th century Lusignan Crusader castles of St Halarion and Buffavento.

These sit perched high above in defensive formation along the Five Finger mountain range in what is now known as the "Turkish Republic Northern Cyprus" - an unrecognised and unloved state that came into existence in 1983 after a brutal civil war between Turkish Cypriots and Greek Cypriots, egged on by Archibishop Makarios and his right-wing Enosis compatriot generals in Athens who were intent of destroying the 1961 Cyprus independence constitutional settlement guaranteed by the British, Greek and Turkish governments.

I first flew into this unrecognised Republic via Istanbul in the Spring of 1987, landing at a small makeshift military airport called Ercan, a few miles from the walled city of Famagusta where Shakespeare set *Othello*.

In flight from both my life in London and a passionate affair, I had decided to take the first overseas job that anyone offered me. It turned out to be as an assistant professorship in political philosophy with Southeastern University, Washington DC, which was helping to establish an international campus in Kyrenia.

Tired and exhausted, I still recall being driven away from suspicious Turkish officials by an English lecturer called Peter across the dusty, barren and brutal plains of Nicosia which separate the Troodos Mountains in Greek Cypriot controlled Cyprus from the five fingers-range in Turkish army control. My mood began to lift as we actually finally passed the giant red flag of Turkey – which had been etched into the countryside by the Turkish army to remind all the Greek Cypriot residents of Nicosia just who controlled what - to reach the summit.

For there, on the other side, stood before me a land transformed – a land of Pine and Cypress trees, of mountain streams and flowers, of olive and lemon groves – with the beautiful Byzantine Abbey and sleepy hilltop village of Bellapais glistening in the distance just above the turquoise sea of the eastern Mediterranean, where thirty years earlier, between 1953-56, Lawrence Durrell worked also as a teacher and wrote *Bitter Lemons*.

Back then, the British were in charge but soon found themselves in the grip of the 'Enosis' terror campaign (Union with Greece), which would eventually tear the country apart and lead to Turkish occupation of the north. *Bitter Lemons* charts the 'feat of unreason' that took hold of the Greek Cypriots in the mid-1950s. Durrell finally fled the country from the same military airport I flew into but without so much as a goodbye to his friends.

By the time I settled in a simple one-storey house surrounded by olive and lemon groves on the outskirts of Kyrenia, the Turkish Cypriots had declared unilateral independence under the watchful eye of the Turks. Yet the old town of Kyrenia still looked and seemed to beat to the rhythm of the British Empire, with its colonial style buildings replete with 1920s post office, green cottage hospital, row of legal chambers and a pro-British money changer called Sargent Mustapha, who had kept the title the Empire had given him.

Every Sunday I would watch a motley crew of left over Empire administrators, who had themselves relocated from India and Kenya, parade past the lemon and olive markets to take Sunday Service at the little 19th century Church of St Andrew's before retiring to the beaten up faded Country Club, where the roasts came with lemons inserted into every orifice.

I would spend the next three years walking and living amongst these lemons, teaching philosophy, drinking in the beautifully kept taverns with colleagues and students, climbing up Crusader castles, exploring the ancient Greek cities of Salamis and Soli, swimming with turtles, visiting Rustem's bookshop in old Nicosia, playing tennis in the wonderfully turned out Nicosia Tennis Club next to the green zone with its barbed wire fences and brutal concrete walls that kept the two populations apart.

Much of this life has now faded away but I'm happy to report that the miraculous old tree in the grounds of Bellapais – just opposite the village square where locals play backgammon into the summer night – still stands and spouts forth both oranges and lemons to the delight of the villager Muktar and the multitude of pilgrims who pay homage to it.

I did not really believe that this was so until I too witnessed the phenomena and its progeny for myself, and in that moment, I too became convinced that Lemons really do have magical qualities.

Part Two: The Darker Side of Bitter Lemons

BUT I would not wish to leave you with the impression that it was all plain sailing in the magical island of Cyprus. Beyond the beauty of the land and its produce, Cyprus, during the 1980s, also had a darker, more elemental side, where the ravages of conflict, war and maladministration allowed warmongers, racketeers and gamblers alike – as well as those just in search of fortune and excess – to ply their trade and wares with little or no official constraint, just as many had done during the civil war in Beirut, which lay just 30 miles across the water.

Like Lebanon, the veneer of government was skin deep, and a lot of people got hurt.

I still retain a crystal-clear memory of finding myself sitting before a Turkish General dressed in all his paraphernalia after he had confiscated my car near an army base on the sweltering Nicosia plains after I had left it to find petrol. As I began negotiations to get the car back, a local Turkish Cypriot peasant burst into the room uninvited – insane with worry – and proceeded to beg the General to help put out a fire that had engulfed his little dwelling in the small village that had been annexed to make way for the Turkish base.

I watched with increasing horror as he was told to sit in the courtyard as the General finished his Köfte, liberally squeezing the last of the juice of his lemon.

"So where are we?" he said with a twinkle in his eye, clearly enjoying my disquiet at his abject demonstration of medieval court power. "And what precisely was in the boot of the car?" he enquired slyly.

I paused as I thought about my new tennis rackets, radio and picnic basket, which I would never now see. "Nothing," I finally answered, as he broke into a huge grin and waved me out exclaiming,"Excellent. You're free to go!"

As I drove off, I looked back to see the peasant abjectly kneeling and kissing the hand of the General as his troops were finally ordered to help the peasant put out the fire on what was left of his home. Perhaps British rule was not so bad in Cyprus after all.

And then there was the teenage orphan with learning difficulties who eked out a living begging from tourists in the harbourside restaurants of Kyrenia. How can I forget the spectacle when – not long after getting my car back – he appeared along the promenade sporting a new linen jacket, evidently given to him by some well-wisher.

He looked so proud of himself until his gleaming smile turned to tears as the local Mafia hoods from the harbour ripped the jacket from his back and began to taunt him as onlookers averted their gaze.

Unable to stand it any longer, I confronted their leader poking my finger at his face. They desisted after other tourists gathered around but I knew there would be a reckoning of sorts. Later that night I went dancing with a German cousin. Within minutes, my younger cousin was surrounded on the dance floor by the thugs from the harbour after they accused him of pushing them.

Once again I sought to intervene but this time the ringleader drew a small knife and flicked it across my face slicing off part of the skin between my eyes. I dropped to the floor as sheets of blood enveloped my own linen suit.

For the next two minutes I was punched and kicked and thought I was going to die until a group of students rescued me and took me to the old cottage hospital where, at 2am in the morning, an old Cypriot nurse sewed my skin together without anaesthetics as I was too drunk to imbibe them.

I left with an eye patch, broken wrist and bruises all over my body. The next day I reported the attack to the local Kyrenia police only to be told that they had opened a file against me as, while I was failing to the ground, I had apparently reached out and touched a girl's skirt.

Undeterred, I repeatedly pressed for a proper investigation. Over the course of the next few weeks, two men in a car followed me as I emerged each morning from the lemon groves to go to and from the University, each taking turns to brandish a gun.

Up until then I never quite understood why in films those under attack never left their homes to seek refuge with others. Now I know.

You can't run forever from your life or hide from a conflict that has not run its course. As John Donne once observed, "Never send to know for whom the bell tolls; it tolls for thee."

So I stayed put and took my complaints to the Prime Minister through an influential gay friend who, by sheer chance, happened to be his chief of staff. That was not before I was advised to go to "Fat Jack" who ran the local casino concessions.

It was solvable, he advised. "But one favour deserves another, Mark, and there may come a time when we might need you to take a little package back to England when you're next going home."

It was a decisive moment for me and the rule of law. I decided to press on with the PM who finally ordered the Nicosia police to investigate. All of a sudden, two suspects were in custody and I was asked to attend an ID parade and identify them from the line by pulling them out by the shoulder.

The experience taught me how the mind plays tricks with the memory under such intense conditions, something which later came in use during cross-examinations at the Old Bailey. Sometime later, after two suspects were identified, a teenage boy rushed into the station to confess to the knifing. He was summarily sentenced to two years in circumstances where I was not informed or required to be in Court. Such was the rule of law in Cyprus. All now considered it honours even, and I was allowed to return to the sunnier side of Cyprus unhindered. However, I never did see that orphan boy again.

Death and misadventure then, were part of the ebb and flow of life in Northern Cyprus. During the three years I lived in Cyprus, 16 people I knew died. One student was decapitated in his open top car after missing a turn off on an unregulated and unprotected hairpin bend. Another lost her life after a pharmacist prescribed penicillin despite her known intolerance to it.

A Scottish friend's father died of lung cancer unable to access proper care due to bureaucratic inertia. A little boy got shot by a soldier trying to retrieve a ball from the Green Zone, as did a mother protesting at the failure of the authorities to disclose the whereabouts of her son who disappeared during the civil war. All without enquiry, and so it went on.

I finally left Cyprus at the end of term in late 1989 as Europe teetered on the brink of revolution. After listening to reports and the noises of insurrection from Romania on the World Service, I decided to hand in my notice and one week later, crossed the Czechoslovak border to join Václav Havel's revolutionaries in Prague and start a completely new life.

But that was not before one last death happened in Cyprus in the remote and infertile panhandle of the Karpaz, just past a military check point by the Apostolos Andreas Monastery where a few old nuns were routinely harassed for their forlorn attempt to keep the Greek Orthodox flame alight.

The death occurred out to sea near a rough rocky outcrop which looks out from the very tip of Cyprus towards the Levant, where John was once crowned by his knights as King of Jerusalem, and the snorkelling was to die for.

It was a death that brought the aristocracy of youth in me to an abrupt end – and it is one which has continued to periodically haunt me. I have little doubt that it needs to be told – but after reflection, not in celebration of Lemons which constitute a beacon of light and hope rather than of darkness and sadness, as exemplified by all our contributions.

But thank you Decameron for taking me back to my past, to that and other moments, and for reminding me to never send to know for whom the bell tolls for in the dead of night, as we look back and reflect, we all know that it invariably tolls for thee.

DJ: Think I'll put *Bitter Lemons* by Lawrence Durrell on my Kindle. Book seems to be out of print?

PW: I enjoyed *Three Singles to Adventure* in the then British Guiana, looking for sloths and such like, Dorothy. I had a distant cousin in Guyana, interesting to read what it might be like to visit there?

MW: When we lived in Garlieston there was as elderly widower who lived along from us - her late husband had been High Commissioner of The Cameroon's and she had been on the expedition – along with her husband – upon which Gerald Durrell based *The Bafut Beagles*. Dorothy, where the Allans rented - it was Mrs Austen..

MW: I ordered the Scottish book you were reading Pat - unfortunately Amazon sent e.mail yesterday saying they had cancelled the order – hope Amazon UK is not going into lockdown like Amazon France... Thankfully have piles of unread books at Kilness.

PW: I start and end my day reading. Will return to Robertson, so much going on first read. Not many books I return to. Going to return to *Man in a Red Coat*. Describes insecurity, anxiety and fear. Somehow also encapsulated hope and survival so far as I remember. Thanks for the cheery video Marie.xx

MW: Pat – Dorothy suggested looking for books on eBay! Have just ordered the Mackay Brown book as well as the Scottish book – looking forward to Wednesday+ for ETA..?

PW: Possibly what is happening with Amazon is staff becoming ill. The packers and delivery workers have been outstanding keeping things going for us all. My neighbour works on the oil rigs and he has been unwell with Covid19. His family are obliged to self-isolate and for me just stay home. Hard with the weather so lovely. I have family, friends, people who help, projects, and this project. Not too much of a hardship X

PW: Everything takes ages to arrive, half the Royal Mail staff have been unwell or self-isolating. Can take twice as long or more for deliveries. But it all arrives. X

PW: I have an array of boxes; everything goes in a box. If I need something soon after arrival ultra-careful. Remove packaging. Wash hands. We would have called this bonkers even just a few weeks ago. COD.

MLBM: Mark, loved your piece. It sparked memories for me. Been near there for a conference on the Phoenicians and being investigative went into the Turkish part and was told I'd never be able to return.(such a contrast after you cross the border) am here so fortunately only a scare tactics for the timid so passport stamped and here I am.

Jonathon Gibbs

IF LIFE GIVES YOU LEMONS, MAKE LEMONADE.

**Wood Engrav-
ing**

**A KNIFE PENETRATES THE BOTTLE TO PIERCE ENTWINED HEARTS. HOWEVER
THE BOTTLE MAY BE EMPTY.**

Andrew Brown

Soor Plums

THE subject of lemons chosen by Marie-Louise over the Easter weekend immediately reminded me of lemon drops, which I loved in my childhood as well as the chemical tasting pear drops and the girn inducting Soor Plooms, all traditional Scottish boiled sweets.

Coming from a Catholic family as soon as we were old enough, we were encouraged to celebrate Lent by denying ourselves some personal pleasure from Ash Wednesday 'till Easter Sunday, such as giving up sugar in tea as a lenten penance which in my case resulted in a permanent and healthy abhorrence of sugary drinks both hot and cold.

Less pious was an abstinence from all sweets and confectionery for lent because along with my brothers and sisters after classes at St Joseph Catholic Primary School in Clarkson, near Glasgow on our way home, we would stop at a sweet shop in a redundant signal box and spent the usual daily pocket money on favourite sweets and taking them home to store in enormous glass jars to be gazed at longingly in their multi-coloured beauty until Easter Sunday, when we would gorge ourselves on our saved treats as well as chocolate Easter eggs and make ourselves thoroughly sick, justified by our saintly self-denial over the past month.

After such indulgence one of the few things I could face over the next couple of days were citric boiled sweets, such as soor plums, invented in, of all places, Galashiels in memory of the 14th century massacre of an English raiding party on the banks of the Tweed, who were overcome by the local lads after becoming ill from eating unripe plums. This story is reminiscent of Michelangelo's lost mural of the Battle of Cascina where a group of Florentine soldiers bathing in the River Arno narrowly escaped a similar fate at the hands of a platoon of Pisans

The Scottish skirmish is supposedly commemorated in the coat-of-arms of the Burgh of Galashiels which includes two foxes looking up at a plum tree with the words "Soor Plooms" inscribed below. However, in reality the motif probably derived from a medieval burgh seal depicting a fox underneath a vine hanging with grapes based not on the Borders legend but on an Aesop's fable where a wily fox unable to reach the juicy fruit, concludes in consolation that the grapes were probably sour anyway.

A typical embodiment of the practical Scottish temperament and a reminder to ourselves in the present predicament that the grass may not always be greener on the other side of this lockdown.

DJ: Very interesting Andrew! We had a sweetie manufacturer in Wishaw and when in school we could smell what they were making!

PW: Some additional kind of child cruelty Dorothy along with warm milk defrosted by the classroom radiator. Soor it was...

DJ: Absolutely! One of my neighbours worked in the factory and on a Friday, she brought home rejects. They were all sorts of bookings stuck together which we broke with a toffee hammer. Sometimes when eating it there was the odd combination of soor plooms, mint cracknels and pear drops! Delicious! 😊

Mark McLeod

SO, this is my contribution. A collage of lemon/yellow snippets from around my flat today entitled "Isolation lemon/yellow" x Interior of my flat. I love sunlight.

CMS: Wow! Straight out of Interiors Magazine and bet it's sooo clean and tidy! Beautiful.

Barbara Dickson

PRACTISING my drawing. I offer lemons as a little group!

AB to BD: Nice but now try adding colour xxx

AB: Camel urine, if you have any available, is the traditional medieval source of yellow.

RM: I don't think there are any camels in Edinburgh's New Town. Of course, I may be wrong.

MMS: Maybe Mark Gorman could provide the right sort of vintage. I have an in with him and could ask....

RM: Is that how you collect camel urine?

MMS: Only in the New Town.

MMS: Camels come in many sizes and disguises - I would always go with the big man's potions.

PW; Image Barbara this is a very lovely drawing. Re. Camels haha . Simple dyes from the kitchen might work as well as watercolours? IN this era of austerity...From Shetland Dye book by Jenni Simmons.

BD: Turmeric maybe? Too dark perhaps. Thanks for helpful and loving comments. ❤

PW: I was thinking turmeric Barbara but yes, a bit strong and taint. Was thinking Alan used all kinds of ingredients including coffee, tea, bleach in his teaching! In his own work he liked to work on coloured ground. Keep going Barbara.

Jessie Ann Matthew

JM: Great stories everyone. This is Jessie on Jonny's phone. I loved Roddy's citron presse story. It reminds me of holidays with my parents in the south of France. Mark's stories are gripping. Well remembered.

My sketch is from Greece. The house we rent has its own little lemon grove, what a treat, an endless supply of lemons, one of life's great enhancers.

Something more banal. Bella's key fob.

SERENDIPITY

Catherine Maxwell Stuart

THIS has never been a word I have used very much and I have found I have kept thinking of many more accidents with unfortunate outcomes than fortunate ones. However, my husband, of course, reminded me that had it not been for a very serendipitous meeting, we may have never re-connected and not been together now.

Mark and I met during our first week at LSE and by the second week had had a brief affair that lasted one short night. However, we had become firm friends since we first met so we continued to see each other all the time including a memorable drive to Traquair with four of us in a Volkswagen Beetle. None of my friends were quite prepared for what loomed out of the darkness when we finally drew up outside the house as I had always been vague about where I lived.

By my second year, I had met Francesca who had quickly become a very close friend and we moved in together into a tiny two-roomed attic above the Monmouth Coffee House. I went to Thailand with her in the summer and skiing with Mark in the winter. Yet our friendship remained platonic, despite sharing a bed for two weeks, rescuing him from a horrid accident and delivering him back to his mother in a wheelchair. Perhaps she did have a soft spot for me after that experience.

In our final year Mark and Francesca met, independently of me, in a lecture, and embarked upon a deep, passionate and tempestuous affair culminating in a wild trip across Turkey and a frantic call to me from Francesca asking me to witness their marriage in Cardiff.

I am not exactly sure why I turned them down. They were my two closest friends but I was convinced it was a bad idea and I just couldn't bring myself to be part of it.

Fast forward a year and I am working in Bristol for a theatre company. Mark and Francesca had lived in London for around 9 months before the relationship exploded and Mark left for Cyprus. I was still in close contact with Francesca who spent many hours on the phone as we indulged in general anti-men raging.

She told me that Mark was not interested in seeing me which I believed not having heard a word from him since he had left London, assuming he had just treated our friendship as a passing university dalliance.

Then, about a further eighteen months later I was at Francesca's flat and having a meal when the doorbell rang. By this time Mark was back from Cyprus and they were back on reasonably good terms. Francesca, I knew, clearly hoped they might get back together.

I remember hearing Mark's voice as he walked up the stairs and I froze wondering what sort of reception I was going to receive. He looked just about as startled to see me. Weirdly though, I sensed there was no animosity and it seemed a natural resumption of our friendship.

Francesca seemed a little taken aback but there was little she could do about it. It was clear she felt she could only be in control of both of us If she kept us apart.

I later learned that she had told Mark that I was no longer interested in pursuing my friendship with him. Our relationship resumed after that night although it was a further ten years before we finally got together.

Yet had it not been for that serendipitous meeting, it is quite possible we would never have reconnected.

RM: Very moving. Such is life and such is serendipity.

DJ: Lovely piece Catherine.

CS: Lovely Catherine x

BD: I love the twist and turns of life as indicated here by Catherine.

MLM: I took a deep breath Catherine. Reliving this with you. I hope you eliminated Francesca from your phone book.

AB: Such a pity Francesca couldn't deal with it but despite her machinations all ended happily ever after.

Mark Muller Stuart

TWO small moments of serendipity to report from last week. One on Friday when under the strain of a beautiful warm spring day – set against an impossibly blue sky – my resolve to abide by the lockdown nearly broke in favour of sharing a chilled glass of white wine up at the Glen with Andrew.

Somehow I managed to resist the temptation and keep on the right side of the law by going for a swim in the river instead, only then to take a call from Andrew who by sheer chance was on his way back from Sainsbury's with a bottle of Picpul de Pinet.

It was then that a cunning plan was hatched. Each of us would go to a side of the River Tweed whereupon we would both swim to the centre and meet two metres apart and then go to a point along the river where we would partake of the bottle chilled by the natural currents of the Quair, courtesy of three glasses brought to the confluence of both waters by Catherine.

And so it came to pass – evidenced by the two photos attached – as a series of accidental and coincidental events came together to result in an outcome of mutual benefit to us all in what I call **SERENDIPITY 1**.

SERENDIPITY 2 was a little stranger and opaque. It occurred early this morning in the form of a dream.

Throughout the previous day I had been researching the letters and archives of Traquair in order to better understand the history and life of the house in the 1770s for a book I am writing about a Virginian law student Cyrus Griffin, who came to Traquair at the invitation of Lord Linton in 1770, only to elope with his sister, the eldest daughter of the 6th Earl of Traquair, to the revolutionary colonies of America where, over time, he became the 10th President of the Continental Congress of the 13 States of America.

There, he handed power over to the first President of the United States, George Washington, in April 1789, after the ratification of the Constitution on the United States.

Last night I went to sleep filled with a multitude of new insights about the history of the house and its past inhabitants – including learning that the downstairs toilet we all use during dinners at Beyond Borders was once a little prison which in 1628 incarcerated a 'Gypsy' called Patrick Faw.

Suddenly all sorts of images from the house began to filter through my mind as I slipped deeper and deeper into a Rem dream, until I finally elided upon a set of hidden secret artefacts, which had evidently been kept back from public view.

After polishing the disparate pieces that consisted of buckles, a leather pouch and some straps, I rushed to Catherine to tell her about this remarkable new find, but unaccountably she seemed totally uninterested.

After some further research I discovered that these artefacts did not in fact emanate from Catholic Traquair but came to it through her mother, Flora's Jewish line of the family stretching back to the Duke of Lasada who was forced to flee Spain after the Spanish Inquisition.

So this time I rushed to Flora but she also seemed utterly underwhelmed. Perplexed by the responses, I stared down at the artefacts to try to understand their lack of interest but also meaning. As I moved the artefacts around like pieces in a jigsaw, they suddenly aligned into something that took my breath away.

There before me lay two 15th century leather masks. It then dawned upon me that they had been successfully used to protect their owners from a European plague some five hundred years ago.

It was then that I woke up to find Catherine gently sleeping by my side. It was all a dream but somehow those artefacts remained with me all day. Twelve hours later I discovered that I had tested negative in an anti-body test for Coronavirus and would have to remain vigilant for the foreseeable future. Yet somehow the serendipitous images of these two old masks lifted the spirits and gave me hope in the ingenuity and capacity of mankind to persevere and survive.

Cyrus Griffin

Christine Stuart

RM: Fascinating Mark. I was told by one of my editors never to use the word "new". There is no such thing as "new", he insisted. When I wrote my East Lothian book, I discovered two of my ancestors who farmed at Morham both died of the plague within a week of each other in 1580.

JM: Great pieces Callum and Mark. Envious of your dip. We have been immersing in our local burn, only get about six strokes though.

BD: Mark, the name Faw or Faa was usually applied to gypsies. Fascinating stories.

MMS: Well how extraordinary this all is.

AB: I have several old photos of the last king of the Scottish gypsies and his cottage in Yetholm. Still known as "Gypsy Palace"

CMS: I have a book somewhere with photos of Yetholm and the gipsies.   Eddie Cockburn who used to live at Yetholm told me many strange stories of the gypsies there. Through his Yetholm horse dealing contacts I bought my most amazing pony - he came with the name Western Gamester.

AB: Do try to find it Catherine and are you sure that the Patrick Faa who was imprisoned at Traquair wasn't this one who was transported to America in 1730s.

PW: Andrew, the story of the Gypsy Palace is fascinating along with the photos. Thank you for sharing.

My Granny Agnes Dyer lived in Pitlochry. She used to talk about growing up in Pitlochry and never needing to lock their door not even when the gypsies came by, they never touched a thing. But I also understood from her you must buy their wares. She was born in 1887. Also, my mother would always support any traveling people who came by as did Alan and me. When we lived in Ladybank a most helpful service was from the traveller who came each spring to sharpen our gardening tools.

La Celine

Brief Encounter

On the 4.16 from Iddlesworth
It started with a twitch
And even more absurd
Me skirt I had to hitch
I then came over queer
Me temperature arose
And to my greatest fear
A lump upon my nose
And if that wasn't enough
The disease began to linger
A rash under me cuff
A blister on me finger

Maybe it was the apple crumble
A touch of salmonella
I really mustn't grumble
I'm not a story teller
For how lucky was I
For sitting opposite me
A smiling cheerful gentleman
A doctor definitely

Oh doctor, oh doctor
What could it be
Will I truly die
Me ashes thrown to sea
Oh doctor Oh doctor
will you help me out
I'm due in Rye at 6.30
And I'm feeling like a trout!

And then from out of his case
He produced a tube of cream
He said "rub in three times daily
and be careful not to scream
If the problem still persists
Then take one of these
The side effects are this the
shaking of the knees
and with one of those
The shaking it will stop
The lump upon the nose
will sooner or later drop"

Without further ado
I took the medication
And thanked the doctor as he
got off at the next station

As the train pulled away
The horror really begun
Me body began to sway
What had this bugger done

Oh doctor, oh doctor
What could it be
Will I truly die
Me ashes thrown to sea
Oh doctor, oh doctor
you've really helped me out
I've arrived at Rye at 6.30
And I'm sipping on me stout!

Celine Hispiche

Roddy Martine

SERENDIPITY. Not so harsh as Kismet or the Fickle Finger of Fate. Yes, I believe in Serendipity.

For example, it was serendipity that in the Autumn of 1979 introduced me to – and I give you all permission to laugh – Andrew Brown.

I had recently been loaned a disused cottage at Hopecarton on the Drumelzier estate at Broughton. It had been uninhabited for a few years but was wind and watertight with electricity and a supply of spring water sourced from the Hopecarton Burn streaming from the three Donalds of Pikestone Hill, Middle Hill and Drumelzier Law.

It was idyllic. Never mind that you had to walk across five fields and through five gates, to reach it from the main road or that worms regularly poured out of the kitchen tap.

Basic, simply furnished, surrounded by undulating hills and big skies. I often spent weekends with only the sheep that huddled around it at night for company. I whitewashed the exterior walls, chopped wood for the fire and dug out the burn to create a swimming hole. Instead of writing my great novel as planned, there were always daily distractions. Above all, there was plentiful time for me to just sit and dream and do nothing.

Tweedsmuir remains the heartland of Scottish Arthurian legend where Merlin the Magician is fabled to have found refuge after the Camelot dream came to an end. In this great rolling, tumbling gully of a place where Peeblesshire meets Lanarkshire meets Dumfriesshire, its very remoteness inspires flashbacks of a supernatural nature. You can actually feel the afterlife.

Indeed, the story goes that Merlin himself is entombed inside the trunk of a thorn tree on the river bank, placed there by that wicked but rather sexy enchantress Morgan Le Fay. Then there is the 13th century prophecy of Thomas the Rhymer foretelling that, "When Tweed and Powsail meet at Merlin's grave, Scotland and England shall one monarch have."

On the very day in 1693 when James VI of Scotland crossed over the Border into England, the River Tweed overflowed its banks and joined current with the Powsail Burn, something it has never done before or since.

But I digress...

At that time (1979, not the fifth century), I had a friend called Rebecca Irvine living in London. Rebecca was editor of *Lipstick Magazine* and one day telephoned to ask if she might borrow the cottage to chill out with a girlfriend who had recently returned from the South of France.

On the train journey across France, the girlfriend had shared a carriage with a gallery owner from Edinburgh who had been visiting his partner of the time, the administrator of an arts foundation in Vence. The gallery owner, needless to say was Andrew Brown. Rebecca sounded excited. Her friend, she said, was smitten!

I was editor of *Scottish Field* magazine at the time and I thought I already knew all of the art gallery owners in Edinburgh – I had been a habituate of the Demarco Gallery as a teenager. Then I recalled a darkly intriguing figure, an unkept shoulder shield of thick black hair topping a bottle green suit, that had been pointed out to me lurking on the staircase of the McEwan Hall at the Edinburgh Festival Fringe Party.

"He has invited us to a 2001 party!" Rebecca informed me, adding, as an after-thought, "He says you can come too!"

Well, there you have it. Rebecca and her friend were installed at Hopecarton with supplies for a week and on the Friday night arrived at my flat in Edinburgh. By pure co-incidence, I had another Merlin, this one an old friend who had recently been installed as Hereditary Lord High Constable of Scotland, also staying the night. "He can come too," announced Rebecca.

And so the four of us set off to the 369 Gallery in the High Street. I don't think any of us knew what to expect. The Lord High Constable wore his kilt and when we climbed the stair and entered the gallery, we were welcomed by a voluminous naked woman posing as the planet Saturn, her more than ample proportions shrouded by a thin veil of gauze. Our host was dressed as a Planetarium with wire appendages.

There were projections of abstract paintings on the walls, some a trifle rude. Various gamin boys emerged from the sidelines attired in costumes ranging from very little to military uniforms. It was as if we had stumbled into a Pier Paolo Pasolini film set. And thus I was introduced to Andrew Brown.

The following day, Rebecca and her girlfriend invited him and a few party survivors she had scooped up to Hopecarton for Sunday lunch. The Lord High Constable, still wearing his kilt, headed north to his Aberdeenshire fiefdom but the rest of us, as I recall, barbecued sausages and, for some totally inexplicable reason, drank copious amounts of triple vintage cider beside the Hopecarton Burn.

Serendipity? Yes, I'd say so,

For here we all are four decades later...

Callum Stark

OF the three topics so far, serendipity is certainly the theme that holds most resonance for me. Perhaps that is why it has also been the most difficult to write. Considering the many ways it has influenced my eighteen years, I can say that almost everything truly good has been the product of provenance's kinder sister.

But which aspect to write about? I decided it would be best to think back to the first event of true serendipity which altered the course of the years to follow: my introduction to Edinburgh's Fruitmarket Gallery

One night, aged sixteen, I'd been due to go to a gig with my parents and older brother, until last minute we realised it was 'Over Eighteens Only'.

"If it was in Edinburgh and not Glasgow, we would try and sneak you in; can't have you wandering the Barrowlands though, can we?" my mum said, before promptly driving off.

It being too late to make any proper plans, I was resigned to a night alone. Until I remembered the Fruitmarket Gallery were doing a lecture on a little known performance artist, Lee Lozano.

At this time I didn't hang around galleries a lot, and had wandered into the Fruitmarket for the first time the previous week on a whim and was amazed by a Tacita Dean film I saw. It was then, too, that I had seen, on one of their little pink fliers, that they were giving a lecture.

Except it wasn't a lecture at all. In reality, it was a participatory recreation of one of Lozano's performance art filled evenings, or "Happenings". As I am sure you can imagine, this was a fairly disarming realisation.

I was so intimidated walking in, everyone was sat in a circle and evidently all knew each other. Two grey haired men were in the farthest corner, one wearing tiny round glasses and a black turtle-neck; the other a piece of yellowy-green silk wrapped around himself like the robes Buddhist monks wear. I would later find out that these were Lorenzo's New York art dealers from back in the day.

The performance had already commenced, unbeknown to me, as I was offered by one of the curators, a jar filled with £100 in notes and coins and told to take as much as I liked.

I have to say I have never felt less like a radical performance artist from New York and more likely a 16-year old schoolboy from Edinburgh as I awkwardly fished out a measly 5p from a hat brimming with notes.

Which, in fact, only serves to highlight the perhaps not obvious genius of Lozano's work, which were really experiments which gently prodded at human nature. She recorded meticulously the reactions of all those offered the jar, and their responses cover the full spectrum of human emotion from the indignance of Claire Copley to the gratitude of Arthur Berman who took $20 for the subway to John Toreano who took the jar but no money. Had I visited Lozano's loft in 1969, she would have recorded that "*UPTIGHT 16-YEAR OLD BOY TOOK ONLY 5P BUT WAS LATER PERSUADED TO TAKE £40 TO SPEND HOW HE WISHED*."

I didn't know it, but that evening of performance art marked the start of a lengthy association with the Fruitmarket Gallery. Indeed, I remember bumping in to Fiona Bradley, director of the Fruitmarket, in conversation with a designer I'd worked with on an exhibition at a separate gallery. "You know Callum too?" he asked.

"Excuse me," Fiona replied, "here at the Fruitmarket we like to think we invented Callum."

I would go on to spend many more nights there; I've run workshops there. And through it, I have met several people who have further influenced my creative and personal lives. Indeed, some of the staff have gone on to become dear friends and I was only reminded of this story when having a drink a couple of months ago with Iain, the curator who had originally offered me the jar of money.

Perhaps why we can sometimes forget these acts of serendipity is that, after a while, it seems absurd to think of it being any other way, such profound effects it can have on our lives.

RM: Great piece Callum. I wish you could have been at the 369 in the late 1970s when our friend Mitra knocked nails into blocks of wood as a statement of purpose, and Andrew and Alice Beberman Chute's Furbelows (anatomically correct crocheted body suits) re-enacted tableaux of famous old master nude paintings - Birth of Venus and Dejeuner Sur L'herbe.

CS: Born in the wrong time Roddy!

PW: Thank you for sharing Callum, a great story full of hope.

CS: That is the restaurant where Andy Warhol used to go to get a frozen hot chocolate!

Marie-Louise Brulatour Mills

I could eat in the dining room of our Park Avenue apartment when I was 18 years old. A milestone for others but for me it was a real millstone. I'd rather stay in the kitchen with my Irish nanny, not here at the breakfast table.

Breakfasts with my father were silent except for the scratch of the silver bamboo shaped pen and the crunch of the Thomas protein toast as he scribbled and calculated his last day's earnings derived from the financial pages. I was eighteen years old that day.

Instead of celebrating my eighteenth birthday at my parents' favourite restaurant Jack & Charlie's 21 Club, I invited them out. My mother more generous and more social than my father, knew I had saved up my weekly allowance for this and was game to go out of her routine to please me. My father less open to any new ideas that took him out of his comfort zone reluctantly agreed to accept my invitation.

I wouldn't tell them the name of the restaurant but indicated the address to the taxi driver. It was on the East Side and not far away, 60th between Park and Madison, as I recall.

Unlike their usual watering holes, it was simple place, jacket-less waiters, cloth-less tables, and certainly no dress code for the clientele. In fact it was ordinary in all aspects except for one thing, not apricot soufflé but apricot smush (a puree of apricots with heavy cream). yum.

Mother, at home in Buckingham Palace or Madison Square Garden where I rode annually in the International Horse Show, was raised between Paris and New York and sophisticated My father, on the other hand, only spoke English and despite frequent trips abroad to Italy and Japan, primarily for work as the VIP of J.C. Penney Company, had a rather limited view of the world.

Yes, it was my 18th birthday and it was my choice and treat this year.

Serendipity, and the concept behind this magical word, guided me through life. Things are put in front of you. Take it and make it vibrate as it guides you into another realm but you must be willing to go on that journey. Mother was.

Barbara Dickson

I'VE been wracking my brains since Roddy came up with Serendipity as the latest subject for contemplation here on the top of our mountain.

I thought until yesterday that serendipity had never happened, ever, to me, in my entire life and everything could be explained otherwise. It simply was never serendipity. However, I'm sitting amongst it now, without having realised.

I tell my audiences that my original songs have longer gestation periods than elephants. That it takes forever for me to finish songs and always has. My friends make albums and complete a tour while I'm struggling away with my lyrics for the latest song.

Things have been better in the last 5 years or so and I have written four songs in that time (smiley face), but towards the end of 2019, I was bubbling away with three ideas, mainly musical, bits of tunes on guitar and piano, on rough IPhone demos here at home. In February, they were two-thirds done, but by no means complete and the lyrics half done.

Cut to lockdown. Because of having no distractions to speak of. 'deadlines' of all sorts, some imaginary, both family and career, and being pulled hither and thither, suddenly I found myself able to concentrate properly.

With concentration comes the flow of ideas I need to work musically with the result that I have three finished songs. 'Lammas Moon', 'The Real You' and, just this week, 'Goodnight, I'm Going Home.'

The upside of lockdown has serendipitously added to my catalogue of songs. They're in a queue for my next album, as the current one is coming together without them. I've never been in this position in my musical life.

PW: Barbara, what an amazing thing to have been part of.

Andrew Brown

The Ghost of Hopecarton

RODDY'S story of the serendipity of our meeting and his mention of the supernatural quality of the Upper Tweed Valley around his cottage at Hopecarton adjacent to Merlindale reminded me of the strange events a year or so after my first visit to his cottage. That was in 1980 when I had a deadline to write a catalogue introduction for an exhibition of the paintings of Robert Colquhoun, which I had curated for the Edinburgh City Art Centre.

Like Douglas Adams, author of *The Hitchhiker's Guide to the Galaxy*, who rented Glen at Innerleithen every New Year, we both liked deadlines, especially the sound of them whooshing past.

However, in this case, publication of the catalogue was fixed and in order to fulfil my obligations, I decided to self-isolate for a week in Roddy's remote cottage at Hopecarton.

It was Spring but before the clocks had gone forward and there were still drifts of snow in the shadows of the drystone dykes, and it was dark at 6.30 in the evening. The cottage had electricity but no telephone and remember that this was before mobile phones and it was miles away from the nearest habitation and half-a-mile from the main road across several fields and flooded burns.

So Roddy dropped me off with an ample supply of provisions and firewood for the week, including, I remember, several tinned Fraybentos steak pies, Heinz baked beans, After Eight mints, and a crate of wine.

He left to cross the soggy fields before it got dark and I lit a roaring fire and made myself comfy with my books and a tartan rug over my shoulders. Suddenly, there was a deafening knocking at the front door of the cottage – BANG, BANG, BANG, BANG.

Silly Roddy, I thought he must have forgotten his car keys so I walked through the tiny hallway and opened the front door and to my surprise, no-one was there. I picked up a torch and shone the strong flash light over the snowy garden, and then walked round to the kitchen door expecting to find him there. But there was no sign of anyone, and no footprints apart from my own in the snow. A little disconcerted, I went back indoors, securely locked everything and put the noise down to a freak gust of wind.

The following evening at the same time, just as it got dark, the knocking began again, louder than before. So I rushed to the door, threw it open, only to find once more an empty porch. I shone the flash-light over the surrounding fields, but no one was in sight and there were no fresh footprints in the snow.

Now I was beginning to get worried. Was this a bored shepherd from the farm a couple of miles away playing a practical joke on a towny, or perhaps, as Roddy seemed to suggest, a supernatural phenomenon.

The following evening I was ready and waiting and as soon as I heard the knocking, I crept out the back door, rushed round the house and lit up the front porch with my torch and there, looking just as surprised as me, was an enormous white mountain hare knocking its legs against the wooden door in an attempt to keep warm.

A moment later, the frightened creature shot off into the white fields becoming instantly invisible and leaving the most delicate of paw marks on the snow.

So the mystery of the Hopecarton ghost was solved and after that brief face-off, sadly, he never bothered me again though I would happily have shared my lodgings with him so long as he stopped that infernal banging.

RM: What I didn't tell you Andrew is that I was later told by a funny old lady in the village that Jimmy Brown, the shepherd who once lived in the cottage, had got himself into trouble with a local necromancer - there are several in the Tweed Valley (notably Walter Scott the Wizard) – and he had been turned into a large white hare.

PW: Ghost story evenings are so funXxxx

AB: I'm sure you are making that up but it reminded me of Hogg's story of the witches of Traquair which was based on real 17 century witch trial documents in the burgh records of Peebles in which the central warlock who incidentally lived in the now abandoned village of Fethan at The Glen was accused of turning himself into a hare at night so perhaps it was a supernatural visitation after all

RM: In my book Supernatural Scotland there is the story of a disagreeable old woman living in a Highland village. One day a local lad goes off with his gun and shoots a hare in its leg. It escapes but the following day, the disagreeable old old lady is seen walking around the village with a limp.

Dorothy Jackson

WHEN I first heard that Serendipity was the next theme, I did wonder how to approach this. I thought of the big things in my life, and when I heard talk of first meetings of people we are still friends with many years ago, I decided to speak with my oldest friend.

She believed that serendipity might mean chance, fate, kismet, accident or good fortune but too many words for this event to be just coincidence or coming about without any purpose or reason, she believed. How true.

I first met Hazel over 50 years ago. We were at the same secondary school but not in the same class. We met up because her friend had a friend in my class, so at break times we would gather in the cloakroom area, and me being the sociable person I still am (she said this), chatted to all of us.

But that was quite unusual because as First Year pupils we tended to stick to our own classmates. For the next five years, our paths crossed throughout our school days, at breaks and lunchtime.

Hazel left school after 5 years. I stayed on for Sixth Year. We lost contact but, a year later, on the train home from college, I met Hazel. She was at University. Serendipity? We met regularly on the train to and from Glasgow for the next 2 years.

Being a year ahead of me, Hazel moved on to Teacher Training College and then to Lanark Grammar School. Again, we lost contact as there were no mobile phones or computers then!

Two years after our last contact, I was appointed to the Business Education Department at Lanark Grammar School, and I met Hazel in the corridor on a day visit to my new school. Where was the Business Education Department?

Right next to the Modern Languages Department where Hazel worked! Serendipity!

And the contact has never been broken since that day, 43 years ago. We have shared secrets, sorrows, happy occasions, families and children. Hazel's daughter is my godchild. Hazel is the like-minded spirit who knows how to be a true friend, there when we need one another.

Hazel's husband was in my husband Billy's year at school and I met Billy when he joined the Ski Club that I was a member of. He was wearing a Lanark Curling Club sweater and I saw this and said that I knew Hazel and Charlie (who were curlers) and that I had applied to join the Curling Club, I took part in the final game of the year and from then on, Billy and I were a couple.

Billy met Andrew Brown when he was on holiday in Garlieston where Andrew stayed at the time. He had a friend called Bernard who was at school with Alistair who was holidaying with Billy. They connected from that day and 53 years later Billy and Andrew are still friends. As am I!

They have never had a cross word and both Billy and I have relished the friendship. Serendipity!

Sunset – Pat Watson

Pat Watson

FOR me, Serendipity is yin and yang, positive and negative, good coming out of bad. I met my husband Alan in the spring of 1984 when visiting my parents' home. My mother was seriously ill and in hospital. Alan was a neighbour and had popped in to see if my brother was up for going out for some beers.

We fell in love and lived our lives together until late February 2019 when he too died of cancer, not long after the opening of 369 Remembered exhibition at Summerhall. Our son facilitated Alan making it to the opening of the show and also to revisit the exhibition on 21st February, the last time he met with Andrew. I remember Alan telling Andrew that day how much he valued Andrew and his contribution to promoting Scottish art. But for serendipity, Alan might not have been part of 369 Remembered.

The story began in 2009, the year of our son's 23rd birthday. We noticed a Martin Rayner had been consigned for auction. Alan decided to see if he could acquire it for Donald but the work sold for considerably more than we had budgeted. However, the next painting consigned to this auction was listed as a David Cook.

It was an abstract head. Alan recognised it. He headed straight down to their office. "You cannot sell that as a David Cook because I painted it and I am Alan Watson," he told them.

The auction house insisted on provenance so home he came, found the slide, and returned to Edinburgh. The auction house accepted the work was his. The painting had been reframed in a way that obscured his signature. We discussed all of this and I offered to create a website for his art works' provenance, which we launched in 2010. https://alanwatsonartist.com.

Continuing to January 1919, Andrew had been looking on-line for Alan for the *369 Remembered – The Men* exhibition. He had lost Alan's contact details, he didn't find Alan on Facebook (Alan had no interest in Facebook) but he did find the website. Alan was delighted for him to show the 3 large drawings from the Navigatio series in the exhibition. 'Paul the Hermit', 'The Promised Land of the Saints' and 'Jasconius' were wrapped and good to go.

Being part of 369 Remembered meant a great deal to Alan. He loved catching up with old friends and meeting new people too. The exhibition and *The Times* review on the Monday following the opening boosted his confidence a great deal "What's going on? It's like old times...

The Promised Land of the Saints by Alan Watson, 2016.

When Alan died, Andrew worked with me and my family to curate a memorial retrospective exhibition of Alan's work which opened in Summerhall in April last year. He also supported me with curating and hanging a memorial exhibition at Duncan of Jordanstone College of Art in September. We became friends. My heartfelt thanks Andrew and to all of you who supported the exhibitions. Serendipity.

It took Alan 10 years to complete The Promised Land of the Saints drawing. When he finally came up with the idea to complete the composition, it didn't take too much time. The drawing depicts the end of Brendan's epic voyage across the Atlantic in a curragh. An extreme pilgrimage. They had caught sight of the coast of America. Conte and pastel on a coloured ground paper,6X5 feet.

Marie Weir

SERENDIPITY – I know what it means but how to explain it. As I do with all my pupils, use a dictionary. Well, not having a dictionary to hand without going to my study, I did what all pupils do and 'googled' it.

According to the Cambridge English Dictionary, Serendipity – apart from being a girl's name – meaning unexpected good fortune. SERENDIPITY: The occurrence of finding valuable or agreeable tidings not sought for – definitely in my case, READING (at all times and anything).

As the second eldest child growing up in my elder brother's shadow, I followed his reading books in P1 – Janet and John, Tip and Mitten, etc, through to 'Katie the Little Red Tractor' in P2. I remember clearly when I could first read on my own: just after the reading book which contained the story of the seven Chinese brothers who each had a memorable talent to help their youngest brother stand the extreme heat of the Chinese Emperor's oven.

I devoured books whenever I could get hold of them – weekly Wednesday afternoon trips to the library where I loved the 'Madeleine' series of books where I couldn't understand the boy named Jean – a girl's name in Scotland.

After the war, there was little money to spend so I was starved of books and resorted to reading my father's weekly fishing magazine *Rod and Line* – I don't remember learning about fly fishing but it was a read!

What a great joy – and treasure trove – when I discovered Agatha Christie within a suitcase in a cupboard in Netherlee. *Death in The Clouds* was my introduction to Christie and since then murder mysteries are an easy read and an escape when I need an undemanding book!

I adore books and reading as I can learn so much – but my favourite author?

So many – I thoroughly love Edith Wharton, Stevenson, Sir Walter Scott, Willa Catha, any Virago, etc. And the list goes on and on.

However, I must finish a book no matter my disengagement. I discovered one of my favourite author's novels within the Millennium Collection which I had never heard of. *Princess Casamia* by Henry Miller, which took me about 14 years to read – I started so I must finish!

Back to Serendipity – 'books I love; reading I adore.' What a wealth of information one can learn.

Jonathan Gibbs

THIS oil painting is entitled 'I said you said' and measures 26 x 40cm. This was made without any kind of sketch or preparatory studies and was resolved by the process of invention and accident. Whether or not the image is a happy and unexpected discovery may be discussed.

It is an abstraction, and the title refers to a game, conversation, or relationship in which there are different layers of meaning. Serendipity is the faculty of making happy & unexpected discoveries by accident. Related to this definition, Hugh Walpole also said that "the wisest prophets make sure of the event first."

Artists have employed chance, accident or the unexpected, or have tried to. Henri Michaux drew without thinking, as did André Masson. Drink & drugs can help to reduce forethought and planning, although Paul Klee just took his dog for a walk. Sorry, his line for a walk. What can possibly go right, really?

During the walk one's companion, or whatever was on the end of the leash, might do something unpredictable. Of course, accidents will happen willy-nilly or with pre-ordained structures. intuition plays its part in the avoidance of accidents.

And spontaneity often results in something unexpected and indeed happy. Art students are encouraged to apply this principle, whilst at the same time to be rigorously analytical. You can't have it both ways.

And musical improvisation is reckoned to be important, even within J.S. Bach's work.

During a Miles Davis concert of jazz music, as Davis stood back from the band during the various solos, he was asked when John Coltrane's long and convoluted improvisation on the saxophone would end?

He answered, "when he's finished man."

DJ: Very interesting!

AB: Great contribution Jonny Paul Klee was also asked how he knew when a painting was finished and replied when it looks back at you.

Jessie Ann Matthew

I took this shot in Hyde Park in 1975. I was walking through and just happened to come across this teacher exercising with her pupils. It ended up being one of the main photographs in The Quality of Life, the opening exhibition at the National Theatre in 1976 and was used as the front-piece of the catalogue.

DJ: I love the expressions on the kids' faces when you look up close.

RM: Great pic Jessie x

BD: It's a wonderful photograph. It seems such a dated activity now, doesn't it

FIRST LOVE

Roddy Martine

I am reminded of Rosebud in Orson Welles' film *Citizen Kane.*

However, Rosebud was a pony. I have to confess that my first love was a bush baby.

For those of you who have no idea what a bush baby is, let me explain. They are marsupials which originate from the jungles of Zimbabwe: small furry nocturnal animals with long bushy tails, tiny human-like fingers and enormous orange-brown eyes.

And I do often feel guilty about Tichowana because he came to me as a tiny baby via the pet department of Harrods. Then I reassure myself that he had a good life. He was well fed, met interesting people and assuredly outlived most of his family back in what was then Rhodesia by at least three or four years – almost double in bushbaby lives.

Bushbabies sleep during the day and wake up in the early evening as darkness falls. They live on fruit and insects, and Tichowana especially liked to chase large moths.

At the time, my parents owned a house called Cullompton in the leafy green Surrey village of Ashtead, and there was a large conservatory on one side in which Tichowana slept during the day. When I scampered about the house, he liked to sit on my shoulder. He never fell off. When I went to bed, I'd let him loose in my bedroom and he would bounce around, jumping onto the wardrobes, dressing table and window sill. When I woke up in the morning, I'd find him curled up and sound asleep in my dressing gown pocket.

Three years ago I wrote a children's book, a work of fiction called *Tichowana The Bushbaby - A Tail of Three Continents.* Essentially this was an essay on how cruel it is to keep wild animals in captivity.

He travelled to Scotland with me in my overcoat pocket when my parents decided to re-locate to Edinburgh. While they were house hunting, we all stayed first in the Roxburghe Hotel in Charlotte Square, then the Braids Hills Hotel. Both were welcoming to pets or perhaps we didn't tell them.

I began school at Edinburgh Academy and my parents travelled south to organise the move north, taking Tichowana with them. Then came the phone call.

Tichowana had died in his sleep. I was devastated. Something had gone from my life that could never be replaced.

Tichowana was buried under a large willow tree on the front lawn of Cullompton which, when sold, became a retirement home. A small cross marked the spot and a few years ago, one of my sisters returned to have a look at the old place. What particularly touched me was that she told me that somebody, probably one of the residents, had placed a small bunch of flowers on Tichowana's grave.

RM: I write that Rosebud was a pony, however Rosebud was a sled.

RM: First, although I did have a Chinese amah in Sarawak and was heartbroken when my parents brought me home to Scotland when I was six. In later life, I certainly learned the difference between infatuation (as Callum so rightly observes) and genuine unconditional love. I always think of Auden: 'If equal affection cannot be, let the more loving one be me. Admirer as I think I am of stars that do not give a damn, I cannot, now I see them, say I missed one terribly all day.

CS: Loved your piece Roddy - I 'd have loved to meet any parents who would think of such a left field pet. I wonder if Harrods still has a pet department?

PW: Oh dear!

RM: There was a time when you could buy any animal in the world in the Harrod's Pet Department, from a saber tooth tiger to a turtle. It closed in 2014 in favour of a women's fashion floor! Not that I approve of wild animals being kept in captivity but nobody really thought like that at the time. It was an amazing place to go and see what they had.

BD: Far be it for me, Roddy, to suggest little Tich was the only one in your life. However, I think you admit he was the 'first love'!

CS: An apter quote there has never been Roddy!

BD – *Corinthians*. The most beautiful words written about love. Not my offering but further to Andrew, Roddy and Callum.

AB: True Barbara there is the whole essence of Christianity but sadly ignored by so many Christians

BD: It certainly doesn't negate its message. Man is flawed. Bx

ML: Agreed Barbara.

RM: Love is a many splendid thing. It's the April rose that only grows in the early Spring. Love is nature's way of giving a reason to be living. The golden crown that makes a man a King. Once on a high and windy hill. In the morning mist two lovers kissed and the world stood still. Then your fingers touched my lonely heart and taught it how to sing Yes, true love is a many splendorous thing.   Ouch!. Book by Han Suyin. Film- Jennifer Jones and William Holden.

DJ: I used to cry every time this was on TV! Of course, I had to watch it each time. I remember watching it with my mother.

AB: Despite all his philandering or maybe because of it, Burns puts it perfectly especially the lines 'till all the seas go dry and the rocks melt with the sun.' He was a friend of Hutton the father of geology. Who would have thought you could have included the results of a contentious scientific treatise in a love song?

RM: And on the same tack: 'Had we never lov'd sae kindly, Had we never love'd sae blindly. Never met- or never parted, we had ne'er been broken- hearted.'

BD: I'd never noticed before how lovely those words are, Roddy!

RM: I've always considered *Ae Fond Kiss* to be the greatest love song ever written, Barbara. x

Jessie Ann Matthew

band over my first loves!

WHITE Bear belongs to Alexander, our middle son, who would never be parted from him. He travelled everywhere with him from birth to teenage years when he was banned from leaving the house as it was so stressful!

Many times he was lost and returned in bear shaped packages, including from Ikea Liverpool, Humbie to Gloucestershire, the port in Marseilles and the bus on the Greek island of Sifnos (the last two times fortunately retrieved before he went home). So a well and truly loved companion after 32 years!

I thought it best not to embarrass my hus-

Callum Stark

FIRST love. I feel the disadvantage of age acutely for this one. Eighteen year olds are rarely of much authority on the subject. However, whilst I cannot write of love I can of infatuation.

It's a feeling far less illusive than love (it's not limited to puppies), and can often look, and feel like it. To an inexperienced mind, any mind in fact, it can be convincing in the extreme; a mask of dopamine that makes us oblivious to flaws of our wouldbe beloved. Even the most tangential of thoughts are an excuse to think of them. They're resident in your brain from dawn till dusk and often in between, in your dreams, such is the grip. Oh, it can be heady bliss.

But it's not love. Don't get me wrong, limerence can be sweet – but it's not love. And there will be a time – weeks, months, or years after the initial attraction – when you realise that you've been able to think of hotdogs, or Walter Scott, or the colour purple without thinking of *them.*

For infatuation is the costume jewellery of amours, and day by day the mask will be lifted and your desired's numerous faults will become clear for the first time. And finally you'll see in blinding light that what you were feeling was not love, nor anything even close.

And you'll kick yourself for thinking it was. It's like looking back on old photographs, wondering how you possibly could have thought *those* jeans or *that* haircut was cool.

So for now, whilst I write of infatuation and infatuation alone, in a year, or maybe ten, or maybe twenty, I might just be able to write of love.

RM: Impressive Callum. Love means never having to say you're sorry. Alas, that dates me!!

A B: A lesson to us all Callum no matter how old! Ps as you were the first to reply to Barbara's theme you get to choose the next one on 11 May xxx Andrew

PW: What a lovely contribution Callum. Very thoughtful.

BD: If only I'd known the difference when I was young.

Catherine Maxwell Stuart

Baby Blue

AB: The peacock certainly looks impressed Catherine or is it photo-bombing your father?

IT was a mini-van named *Baby Blue* given to me by my father when I finally passed my driving test aged 21.

My relationship with mini vans had started some years earlier with the first Traquair House brewery van that my father had proudly emblazoned with the logo on the side. He loved that van although he had to fold himself almost double to get into it. He would stack up a few cases in the back and go off to make his deliveries.

The body work of mini vans was never great and the floor gradually rusted away so he arrived back on one occasion complaining how he had driven over the Forth Road Bridge in high winds being blown from side to side and ankle deep in water. On another occasion we were late for school so we shot off at high speed to the village with me in the back. The back door didn't close properly and as we sped over the hump back bridge I rolled out, happily unharmed, but it took my father a couple of minutes to realise I wasn't there.

It was, of course, the car I first learnt to drive although when my father took me out, he would spend much of the time making involuntary grabs onto the door handle, so I would persuade a friend to come with me instead. My confidence quickly outgrew my abilities until inevitably one New Year's Eve, I missed a corner and somersaulted down a banking, narrowly missing a concrete post and ending up vertically in a ditch.

Amazingly, neither I nor the passengers were hurt but as we climbed out of the windscreen I thought I would perhaps not tell my parents until the following day. A bad idea, as it turned out. Someone let my parents know they had seen the van on its nose before I had a chance to speak to them. I felt crushed and guilt ridden. My father didn't shout at me which made it worse.

That was the last time I was allowed to drive any cars at home and I went off to university without ever taking my driving test. Finally, a couple of years later, I did get round to taking lessons in London and passed first time. I rang to let my parents know and I could tell from my father's voice he had finally forgiven me for destroying his beloved van.

When I came home the following Christmas, sitting outside the house was a bright blue slightly elderly mini van named Baby Blue.

Passing your driving test gives you an extraordinary sense of freedom but actually having a car in which to exercise that freedom is bliss.

I loved that car and together we spent several happy years together. One of the great joys of my van was that it doubled up as a mini camper van (for small people) and I could squeeze an embarrassingly large number of people in the back.

A memorable adventure was to Glastonbury in 1984 when I took Mark's sister, Maria. We somehow managed to blag our way in with the van pretending I was delivering goods to a trade stand. We ended up parked just by the speaker bank on the main stage and stayed all weekend.

Baby Blue grew older and a little less reliable over the years. Her headlights would suddenly go out now and again which was unnerving and the leaks became more plentiful.

Finally, in Bristol, one wet and filthy night I braked suddenly at a roundabout and a car drove into the back of me. It was the end for Baby Blue and my first love and though another mini van replaced her, it was never quite the same.

DJ: I loved your piece Catherine.

BD: Oh Catherine. Lovely memories and I too had a beloved mini. When this one eventually went to scrap, it was like s pet being put to sleep!

DJ: My first car was a 1959 Morris Minor. It was 13 years old when I got it. My dad paid £15 for it and spent a year working on it. It was called Betsy. Happy days in it.

JM: Hi my first car was a yellow mini also from my father. I used to go up and down the country without a second thought.

Latterly with the help of a pair of tights if the fan belt broke which happened on numerous occasions. Happy memories!

DJ: Billy's grandfather's car . Easter 1972. Jim Allan also.

AB: Thanks, I remember it well. Billy and I were both 17 and he had just passed his test xxx

JM: Classic shot!

PW: Lovely Catherine. My first car was a red mini in 1984. I remember driving to Oban in torrential rain to meet Alan returning from St Kilda. The car kept filling up with water, so I stopped every 30 miles or so to bale out the water with the cup from my flask. I made it to Oban. A joyous reunion. Next time I was based in Fife I told my brother about the leak. "There's a bung," he said. "You should have just pulled out the bung!!"

Barbara Dickson

WELL, it could have been a hamster, a budgie, a mouse or a rabbit, all of which we did have, my brother Alistair and I (thankfully not all at once) in our council house near Dunfermline.

The property was a new build 1960s marvellous terraced house with three bedrooms, garden front and back – excellent post-war housing, courtesy of the SSHA. A wonderful initiative for working people, the concept destroyed by Margaret Thatcher. Don't get me started.

No, the first love of my life was Doris Day.

Doris as Calamity Jane is still enough to make me know for certain in my heart that's where a woman belongs, riding shotgun on a stagecoach across the Black Hills of Dakota.

I have recently visited that place and the hills are nothing like those in the movie. They're proper mountains, whereas the grassy topography where everyone is singing on their way to a dance, is more like the South Downs than Indian Territory. I could never understand why Crazy Horse could love and identify with those 'hills', until I too was captivated by them, the real deal. But I digress.

I was 5 when my mother took me to see *Calamity Jane* at the Picture House in Rosyth, where we lived prior to moving to our council house in Dunfermline. We were in Dollytown, which consisted of little houses, in appearance very similar to prefabs, but made of brick; little square residences with grassy gardens where my dad grew veg in the back and we harvested the crab apples from our fruit tree in front for jelly.

My dad worked at Rosyth Dockyard and these houses were provided for the workforce. These unique buildings were ultimately demolished of course as the Ministry of Defence realised the potential of the land.

After seeing that film, I was completely obsessed with the character of Jane. Here was a girl dressed in buckskins, including trousers, with a Union Army hat on her blonde curls and carrying a gun – a total revelation for me, even at that age. I had always felt a little overwhelmed by some of the feminine givens of the 1950s. Those dresses with huge skirts and the polite expectations regarding children's behaviour were, even then, odd to me, when I loved climbing trees and fighting with wooden swords.
I was more of a fan of Sir Lancelot than Debbie Reynolds.

The only part of *Calamity Jane* that bored me was when Jane was encouraged to 'snare' Bill by wearing a flouncy frock and cleaning the house. Oh dear, and Secret Love was not quite my thing but The Deadwood Stage and The Windy City were.

This wonderful and beautifully energetic young woman singing in her crystal-clear voice was just what I needed to be inspired to bigger things in life. Her energy levels were astonishing, and she drank Sarsaparilla, so how could anyone not love her? What, I wondered, was sarsaparilla?

I've always referenced Doris Day as one of my musical influences, but nobody really knows how profound that was, in her cross-dressing role, representing a rather less glamorous role in reality. Jane was, of course, nothing like Doris, but Doris brought her to life for me. She was sensational in that role and I cried when she died recently. She was not the 'apple-pie' girl they tried to make her, as her life attested to. She, like me, didn't like musicals much either!

Coincidentally, I did get to meet Howard Keel who played Wild Bill in the 1970s in London and, of course, melted at his feet, as he was a proper heart-throb with a wonderful singing voice. He was a real film star and I can understand why Calamity put on a dress to seduce him. I would have switched my buckskins for lace too, given half a chance!

DJ: I too loved Doris Day. I also liked her clothes in some of her films with James Garner and Rock Hudson! Loved your contribution. It brought back happy memories.

BD: Thanks Dorothy. I remember so much from that time. Smells too! Barbara x

RM: Great piece Barbara. She was such a star but then so are you!

BD: I loved her, Roddy. Xx

RM: Howard Keel was also magnificent. *Seven Brides for Seven Brothers* was on television recently reminding me of Sobbin' Women! And I loved *Showboat* and *Oklahoma!* However, I never could quite connect with him in Dallas - *And I Love You So* is such a great song but I found it all a bit too schmaltzy in the context of Miss Ellie!

DJ: I was given a stereo radiogram from a lady who was housekeeper to the gentleman who owned the engineering works my father was Works Engineer in. I can still remember the thrill of the LPs of the musicals. *Gigi, Showboat, Carousel* and T*he King and I*. I'm surprised when there is a quiz on tv how I remember those songs. ♫

DJ: So brilliant Barbara - I used to watch *Calamity Jane* at least once a week, every week, and often twice.

CMS: Loved your piece and loved Calamity Jane - used to watch it with my Dad who adored Doris Day!

RM: The late and brilliant A.A. (Adrian) Gill published an hilarious article in the *Sunday Times* in which he said, "I know all the words from all the songs from all those great musicals - *Showboat, The King and I, My Fair Lady, Mary Poppins* etc. "Oh dear," he wrote, "I think I must be Gay!"

CS: I often disagree with his views, Roddy, yet A.A Gill remains one of my favourite writers and his memoir on his alcoholism, *Pour Me*, is one of my favourite books!

RM: He made me laugh a lot which is as much as I can ask of anyone. He once telephoned me for the lowdown on things Scottish for one of his columns.

I have a copy of *Pour Me*. Very sad but bravely written.

BD: It endures! X

One of Oliver (husband's) favourite books. Oliver retells the story of the IRA in Derry on a Sunday. X

PW: Barbara, my parents Fort Augustus, lovely houses built for forestry and then available for hydroelectric scheme. Curious re Oliver's story. Alan lived near Coleraine in the early 70s.

BD: Oliver's story is retold from the AA Gill book mentioned. x

PW: Thank you Barbara, will look into this. x

Pat Watson

I am aged 4, or as my grandson would say, 'My number is 4. What is your number?'

I tell him, 'It is 6 and 3 but you don't have enough hands.'

I am sitting on a fence post in Fort Augustus swinging my legs as children aged 4 do. They are never still.

The early memory is of my mother chatting with our next door neighbour. She is telling our neighbour how lonely I am because all of my friends had started school.

I was born in December and I think the cut-off date must have been August in those days. I did not understand the concept of lonely at that age but at some point not too long after overhearing this conversation, I too found myself at school with my friends Angela and Sylvia.

I don't remember what date I started school but I do remember being there and discovering reading. I loved the readers, starting with Janet and John and Dick and Jane, tracing the letters with my finger. I relished the musty smell of the paper opening up a whole new magical world full of interesting thoughts and ideas. Imagine liking people, playing games, learning about pets, relationships to other people all dressed up in little sugar coated cameos. Nice tidy children and kind parents who were never flustered.

Reading is my first and most enduring love and continues to be an escape from reality for me.

I was the eldest of 6 children so it was often difficult to find time to read books. My mother expected me to help with my siblings. I came across a safe hideaway in a tree where I could read when we moved to Newburgh. *Animal Farm* was a revelation to me. I didn't want to put it down.

Another safe place in this house was the airing cupboard. I always had a torch so I could read my books under the bed covers. I would save any pocket money not spent on sweets for torches.

Not so difficult to find time since I was a teenager. I would have my books in amongst my school work just in case my parents popped in. By this time we were living in Auchtermuchty and there was not much for a teenager to do there.

At one time, I was reading everything the local librarian could find for me on Extra Sensory Perception (ESP) of by Dennis Wheatley. Hardly an education. I should have been reading 19th century British History or worse, Maths! Don't ask me how I ever managed to pass in higher maths. Albeit second time around. My siblings thought I was a 'swat' but my exam results should have told them otherwise.

My husband Alan too loved to read. He was a voracious reader of novels, art books, musicians and artists biographies, anything about St Kilda, North Rona, fishing and whaling, and so on. I have fond memories of him reading to me from Fiann O'Brien at the end of the day when I was weary carrying our children.

This is a strange time and I frequently feel overwhelmed with the sense of the loss of my husband and not being able to visit my children, grandchildren or friends or for them to visit me. Thank goodness there is always a book to turn to at any time of day or night to be transported off to some other world. It never ceases to enchant me we can be so creative with a few lines and curves.

RM: The writer Elizabeth Smart, who was a great friend of mine and Andrew, gave me a copy of *Best of Myles* to read.

PW: Hi Roddy, how did you find '*The Best of Myles*'? Alan's copy has pages bookmarked from 'Bores' including: 'Or 'The Man Who Wouldn't Let A Radio into The House?"

RM: It is some time since I have read it, but Elizabeth obviously loved it. I was writing columns in various newspapers at the time and she was always trying to improve my writing style. I 've never read any of his novels but the Irish wit in this selection was priceless. 'Bores' - acerbic and very funny.

PW: The very idea, no radio!! Alan always went about with his mp3 player: news, plays, sport, music. If he was out in the garden always had to approach him for attention, too busy listening to something. The books are tightly observed and hilarious. Been quite some time since I read them including *The Poor Mouth*, had a look but can't find our copy. Possibly one of our children has it.

RM: Great Dorothy. Books do furnish a room (and our lives).

BD: Dorothy, lovely piece. I remember also, end of term reading of Damon Runyon by Mr Forrest, our English teacher in Dunfermline.

CS: Brilliant Dorothy! *My Family and Other Animals* and *Prime of Miss Jean Brodie* are two of my absolute favorites too! I went to Gillespie's, the school Muriel Spark based it on, still a fair few Jean Brodies roaming the halls!

RM: Give me a girl of impressionable age and she's mine for life! x

DJ: I always tell people that I was born at Wishaw Cross! My family lived above the Horseshoe Bar. There is a song by Peter Nardini at teacher from Wishaw called "I blew a kiss from Wishaw Cross". It's the story of a mother writing to her son who has moved to California. It's content is very local but in these times I can feel her pain – and my son Andrew is only in Oxford.

CMS: Agree with all you say. Infinitely more lasting than an infatuation. BTW beer on the way

DJ: Look what I've got! Billy's already unpacked some. Can't have any until later when he's finished chopping wood with the chainsaw. I, of course, don't have that problem. Cheers!

Marie-Louise Brulatour Mills

I was ten and so was he
A dark and handsome one for me
His strength reflected in his gait
A slow and steady one for my
fate

Others flirted far and wide
But I was the one whom he relied
To be with him strong and tall
He was special after all

We won blue ribbons most of the time
But I knew he wasn't mine
So here began a love story true
I love my animals maybe more than you

Let's forget the men I met
Unlike my animals or pet
Not kind, loyal, true
Perhaps I should live in a zoo!

Marie-Louise in Montecantini, Italy. Photograph: Dylan Don.

Andrew Brown

MY grandmother kept a prayer book in which I had done a rather good drawing on the inside cover of a priest at the altar. I have no memory of doing it but she used to tell people that when I was a toddler accompanying her to Sunday mass, she had given me a pencil and told me to draw something to keep me quiet. After she saw my surprisingly accomplished picture, she realised I was going to be an artist.

However, until the age of 16, I thought I was destined to be a priest and decided to enter a seminary with the ambition of going on to The Scots College in Rome. So my mother arranged for Gordon Joseph (I have never forgotten his name), Bishop of Dumfries and Galloway, to visit us and discuss my vocation. After a cursory cup of tea, my mother left us alone in her front sitting room in which several of my prize winning school artworks were hanging.

He asked me if I was to become a priest, what would I like to be? I immediately replied, of course, I would like to be Pope eventually. He smiled and said though that was a worthy ambition, not everyone can become Pope, and that what he had meant was which branch of the church would I like to enter?

"Oh," I said, "I would like to be a white father missionary in Africa."

"Why would you like that?" he asked, and I explained that I particularly liked the plain white habit and that I'd like to build a mud-brick church for my parishioners and fresco it. Looking a little perplexed, and glancing at my framed still-lives on the wall, he replied, "Your mother says you like art."

"Oh yes," I enthused. "Next to Jesus, I love art. "

Upon which, he stood up and said,"I'm not sure you are cut out for the priesthood. If I were you, I would serve the Lord through your art." So thus at the age of 16, I was given the blessing of a Bishop of the Church and betrothed to Art from that moment onwards, and like the good Catholic I was, I have never since contemplated divorce.

CS: Of all your stories Andrew, this remains perhaps the most shocking x

AB: I in retrospect I think it explains everything about me I discussed it once with Ricky Demarco who had a similar road to Damascus moment but he was less pleased when the Sunday times quoted me calling him John the baptist to my Jesus Christ

Dorothy Jackson

AS an only child I learned self-sufficiency early on – entertainment was a bit limited. We rarely played board games as a family, although my mother did jigsaws which I hated with a passion. Billy says that my lack of ability to find things stems back to my never having played Hunt the Thimble!

Now we come to my first love which changed my life forever – I discovered BOOKS. Through this I entered a new chapter in my life as I consumed every book I could lay my hands on. Over the passage of time my tastes have expanded. I've dipped in and out of genre. For many years I drew a halt at Charles Dickens as my father blamed him for casting a blight on his school days!

I can remember the excitement of getting a new book and also of visiting the public library in Wishaw. Sadly, in the times we live in (pre-Corona-19), where there are severe constraints on the public purse, public libraries are threatened. As are libraries in schools.

Many schools now only have part-time library staff and I feel it is such a waste of this resource. Courses now call for independent research and there is nothing better than the resource of books. The Internet is no substitute. I think the loss of public libraries has a detrimental effect on communities.

My aunt and I had a job on a Saturday to go to the library and choose books for her neighbours and my maternal grandmother (not her mother). I'm still amazed that she was able to remember what books she had already chosen for them!

My aunt was a graduate of Glasgow University and her degree was in English and Languages. She herself had very varied tastes in books and was even a keen reader of *Mills and Boon* books.

She encouraged me to read widely. I worked my way steadily through everything that Enid Blyton wrote. I realise that her work became increasingly controversial from the 1950s onwards, but I can vividly remember being in the library and watching as the librarian stacked her trolley with returned books and the minute she headed to the Enid Blyton section we rushed to get first dibs on the books.

We, as children, just enjoyed the stories with no mind for their literary merits.

One of the exciting parts of my library visit was the added benefit after the visit that we paid to King's Sweet Shop at Wishaw Cross where I got a quarter of 'Seaside Donkeys."

My aunt always said that had it not been for the 2nd World War, she would have liked to have spent a year abroad. She also would have liked to have worked for Thomas Cook. Although she read fiction, she loved travel books. My friend Rosemary knows how keen I am on travel guides and travel writing.

She said that she felt that all books are travel books. When reading a book, we are travelling constantly. Experiencing new adventures and losing ourselves in the words to become that character, perhaps in another land or just allowing us to have a huge adventure experience.

After my eating up lots of what would be described as Junior Fiction, I moved on to more adult books. In the 1960s, there didn't seem to be the genre of Teen Fiction that we have today so my next favourites were Sherlock Holmes and Jane Austin.

After that the great action writers of the 1960s – Alastair Maclean, Hammond Innes, Neville Shute and my absolute favourite, Agatha Christie. Now I have more wide ranging tastes and love visiting book stores. I'm looking forward to getting back to that after lockdown.

It has been said that reading books can reduce stress. I absolutely agree with this as it is a wonderful thing to disappear into a story for even a short time. During this very stressful time I have been so grateful to have plenty of books to entertain and thrill me.

There are also social benefits as it is fun to discuss books. Book Groups are thriving. *Forbes Magazine* stated that 'in a world of Netflix binges and mobile games, getting to crack the spine of a physical book has become a treat.'

My book club does involve the odd glass of wine and I meet with 5 others monthly. They are not people that I meet with on another occasion. It's great fun and it has encouraged me to read books which I perhaps would not have chosen. However, one ot the downsides of this is that sometimes I am disheartened as we discuss the books in depth.

I feel aggrieved when I hear a character reduced to expressions like: 'a good strong character, good use of language, etc.'

Books allow you to form characters in your own mind and sometimes I take ownership of the character. One of the fun things we do in our Book Group is we each imagine who we would have playing the main characters in the book if a film was made of it. It's an interesting exercise when you hear how others visualise them whilst reading.

The librarian in the school I worked in asked the staff to recommend a book that I had really enjoyed and that a pupil might consider reading. The response was very interesting. My suggestion was Gerald Durell's *My Family and Other Animals* (This was long before the television adaptation). My other favourite was Muriel Spark's *The Prime of Miss Jean Brodie* but my friend got in there first and made it her suggestion.

Children (and adults too) love stories. I remember sitting at the back of a class where it was last period on a Friday and the teacher read the class a book. There was silence and this was from a bunch of 13 year olds!

I love everything about books especially the smell of new books! I find it very hard to get rid of many of my books and keep some with the idea that I will re-read them. Who knows? It's a nice thought.

Mark Muller Stuart – First Love

IT appears that Catherine has unleashed an outpouring of emotion towards her four wheeled friends. Sometimes you only fully understand love once you have lost it. I can still recall the physical pain of having to sell my beautiful racing green 1969 hard top convertible Spitfire at the end of university after my mother insisted that I pay back a debt I owed to a friend who helped me buy it in the first place.

That is to say nothing of my '60s green Beetle called Pablo with a small Christmas tree on its top, which Catherine and I trundled up in to Traquair in October of 1983. It took nearly 24 hours to do so but it had a mattress in the back. I can still recall the swirling wind and clouds as I turned the corner in the depth of a moonless night to see the faint outlines of Traquair for the first time.

There was just one light on as Peter opened the old wooden door to welcome us in. He would later take me on a tour of the house where I would become spellbound by the 18th century Italianate library with its classical philosophers looking down from the ceiling above. It was here where I would later read the first editions of Scottish legal scholars like Hume, while preparing for exams to become a Scottish Advocate at the Faculty of Advocates some 17 years later.

But it was not cars that first came into my head when thinking of first loves. No, what came into my mind's eye first was the image of a yellow little budgerigar, one of my first pets.

I was about eight at the time. While it lived with us, I dutifully fed it but was not enraptured by it, until one day I came home and it was gone. When I asked my mother where it was, she told me my father had taken it to the Zoo to give it a better home.

I was suddenly overcome with a profound sense of loss and of something unnatural having happened. I demanded to go and see it. Some time later we went to the Zoo and visited a large cage full of budgerigars.

"There it is," my mother said, pointing at a yellow one.

But it was not our one and I felt real disquiet as for the first time I suspected my mother was not quite telling the truth.

For the next month I literally inundated her with questions about what exactly happened. It was the first time I experienced a sense of injustice and an adult world that now included an element of mendacity. I would not let it lie. The pain of desperately looking for it at the Zoo – when all along she knew it was a forlorn hope – crushed my faith in the best of all possible worlds.

Finally, she had enough and told me that my father had opened the cage and let it fly out after becoming irritated by its constant tweets while trying to watch the news on television. From that moment on, I developed a highly attuned regard for the truth and not to take things at face value by those who exercise authority over you.

I've often wondered whether it played a small part in why I subsequently became a lawyer with a penchant for cross-examination. To this day I'm not sure I was told the whole truth. My father was a kind man who was orphaned in Partition, and then beaten by a guardian. He never laid a finger on me and I can't imagine him acting so cruelly.

But while I can still recall what the bird looked like, I couldn't remember its name. So last night I called my sister who reminded me of it but also of another strange but unrelated incident that happened around the same time that I had completely forgotten.

She recalled how one summer's day while walking back from the local station, we saw a lovely little Indian girl standing in her garden eating an ice cream. She gave us a great big smile but as she did, a white boy came out of the house next door and proceeded to pour a bucket of water over her head. Suddenly her smile turned to tears. It looked as if her soul had been crushed. Back in the early 1970s, there was a lot of blatant racism on the streets of London.

My sister then told me how I proceeded to lure the boy back to the garage at the back of our garden by affecting to be his friend, where I tied him up and threatened to keep him there if he was ever nasty to the girl again. I let him go after he burst into tears and promised never to do it again.

I find it astonishing that I could have forgotten this incident. Once again, Decameron has unearthed some fascinating flashbacks from a different time, but ones which I'm sure must have left their mark on me in some shape or form.

Jonathan Gibbs

IN 1959 at St Mary's Convent in Lowestoft, Mrs Hubbins taught all subjects to a group of twenty or so primary school pupils. As one of these children I very much enjoyed making pictures. I loved this more than anything else: making pictures.

Mrs Hubbins said to my mother, 'I believe that we have an artist here, Mrs Gibbs'.

I only wanted to do art from that time onwards. Within the scope of this love there are many subjects to explore, most of which cannot he expressed in any other way; certainly not in words.

Music or poetry? Perhaps, but these are different modes of expression.

This remained my direction through school, and remains my true course through real life. It is an undefinable love, but quite specific. I sensed it when aged 5 years, and still do so. It is burning bright.

'Enclosures Beside The Sea', oil on wood panel 2020, 30 x 39cm.

A B: Very true Johnny as Marina Abramovitch said you can't become an artist, you are born one. Caroline McNairn and I used to discuss this and she said she had no choice but to be an artist having been born into a family who had been artists for 4 generations

PW: Alan's fisher grandfather x 3 drowned off Lowestoft. The family sold the boat to feed the children, all minors. Star Elick's mother died a few weeks later, his wife a year later. The family continued with fishing until the 1950's. Alan and I visited Lowestoft on our way to Kent a few years ago. The local paper and fisher museum knew about Alexander's death 1878. Interesting coincidence with Johnny's contribution.

PW: Following the herring.

PW: Alan knew about fishing industry. The fishing community understood challenge.

CONTRAST

Roddy Martine

OFF the coast of North Africa is a small archipelago where the sun shines all the year round and, on Gran Canaria, the largest of these Canary Islands, there is a desert beach of imported golden sand called Maspalomas, a haven for wildlife and European tourists, mostly Dutch and German.

Over January, February and March the salt sea wind disrupts the dunes and scatters the sand. Sun worshippers are obliged to take shelter in the countless stone circles built as wind-breaks, and it was in one such adjoining stone circle that I came across Lars and Moira, two middle-aged, middle-girthed naturists, a seemingly ordinary couple.

Seeking solitude and a sun tan, it is not my usual custom to fall into conversation with strangers, especially when In a state of undress. But in this case, it came about almost by accident. A sun hat was blown across the boundary and Moira introduced herself to me as hailing from Bothwell. Lars, she informed me, was from Denmark.

A day or two passed and Moira, as is in the nature of Lanarkshire womanhood, began to confide in me. Some ten years ago she and her best friend Anita had taken a break from their families and signed up for a girly package tour to the Ruby Palais, a gaudy hotel on the Maspalomas beach front. On their first night, dressed up to the nines at the hotel bar, she had caught sight of this handsome single gentleman wearing a yellow shirt and a black and white striped tuxedo. He had asked her to dance and in the days that followed, while Anita became friendly with the waiters, Moira and Lars would escape to the beach and to the very same stone circle which they now occupied.

Lars, Moira informed me, was in the import/export business, cherry brandy or some such liqueur. He was very wealthy, she told me, and on his third marriage. However, Birgitta, his wife, did not enjoy travelling, especially flying and hot sun, preferring the sweeping grey skies over Copenhagen and dinners within the famous restaurants of the Tivoli Gardens.

So Lars and Birgitta came to an understanding. Lars was permitted to go off on business trips without her. When he was away, Birgitta took the children to stay with her parents in Roskilde.

Moira, meanwhile, explained that she was happily married to a bank manager who commuted daily into Glasgow. They had a teenage son who was experiencing gender identity problems and a daughter who was engaged to a policeman. Moira had enrolled as a voluntary part-time tour guide at Chatelherault, near Hamilton, and, three times a week, she joined forces with Janine, the local doctor's wife, to play bridge.

Lowering her voice, Moira confessed she would never have become a naturist in Bothwell. How could she have done so? What would the neighbours have said?

Before returning home that first year, she and Lars had made a pact to return to the Ruby Palais the following year and in the very same week, and they had been doing so ever since. Fortuitously Anita soon after left her husband in Pollokshields and married the owner of the Ruby Palais.

"I can imagine what you must be thinking," said Moira defiantly with a coquettish giggle. "But, you see, I need variety in my life, only a little bit. I love my husband and our kids but this keeps me sane. I need the contrast between here and there."

"Do your family and friends know about this?" I asked, fascinated.

"They never ask. I never tell," replied Moira. "Seamus, my husband, spends all his free time at the golf club and the kids just tell their pals that Mum is away with Aunty Anita in Spain. I don't think any of them have a clue where the Canary Islands are anyway."

"And Lars?"

"Oh, he and his missus have separated. He's retired now and lives here permanently. I'm away home on Sunday but I know he's got another little friend arriving to spend time with him next week. I don't mind at all. It suits us both. You see, we both like the change. It's the contrast that keeps us going."

PW: I hope you changed their names Roddy?

DJ: Excellent Roddy. There's something about us west of Scotland girls. Mean the talking and confiding, of course!

AB: It's a perfect short story and once again he says it's all true!

Pat Watson

REFLECTING back to this time last year I was regularly travelling by bus to Edinburgh to sit in at Alan's memorial exhibition at Summerhall, often accompanied by Andrew and my sister Fiona. Although the circumstance was poignant, the time spent with Andrew and Fiona was often lots of fun. I met interesting people and caught up with people I hadn't seen for a long time. It all meant a great deal to me.

Contrast with now, the world has a pandemic and people are not permitted to meet.

At the start of the Second World War, my father was living in Dundee. He lived in a flat in Blackness Road. In 1939, my father aged 10 and two of his sisters were evacuated to Aberdeenshire. They were with the contingent of children that were taken by train to Montrose and then allocated accommodation from there. They were sent to stay on a farm in Aberdeenshire. They were quite comfortable there but when the farmer's wife became pregnant she said she could no longer look after my father and his sisters. My father commented she was nice but she hadn't really wanted them.

The second family they were sent to stay with in Aberdeenshire were by all accounts, cruel. My father's sister managed to get a note home to her mother asking if they could come home? When my Granny received the note, she immediately set off to Aberdeenshire to collect her children and bring them home to Dundee.

One time chatting to my father about the air raids I asked him if he had to go to school the following day? He told me Hitler's idea was to disrupt their lives and they were not going to let him so they went to school even if they had been awake most of the night.

Contrast with COVID-19 and how it has disrupted all our lives. It is a disease that interferes with people being able to be with each other, with the people we love. This virus is proving to be a disruptive and ferocious menace.

Marie-Louise Brulatour Mills

Dye

Mike brought me hair dye
I know it's such a lie
Sounds like some sci-fi
I call it a lie for good reason

To some that could a treason
But I pray it lasts a season
I'm so concerned to get it right
The box of red seems too bright

To me all I know is what I see
The white has gone so whoppy
Also all those liver spots
They make my stomach turn in knots

Damn so much we must do
To pretend we must pursue
To make us so much prettier
We try to be so much wittier

Anything we can do to change
A regrowth white, such a pain
To go from plain Jane
to rehaired flame

I am not to blame
I want to enhance my game
The only way seems to be
Get a box of colour and see

If that will make a difference now
or will I just say holy cow
When the colour dries on me
I'll close my eyes and hope to see

Someone looking great
Despite my age and gait
But I'll know so very soon
When I mirror look and swoon

The grey is gone once and for all
But I know not true at all
I'll hassle again with colour dye.
And make a mess and cry

The towels red and strained so much
I now have to bleach it such
To make it white is a pain
But to get my red hair is just a stain

I'll tell myself this is the fact
And look at me and look back
When time gone by I didn't need
To dye my hair was not my creed

But then I didn't need to lie
There wasn't even any hair dye
But I was young and busy so
Even if I had places to go

Time has passed and yet again
I now must so fend
I try to understand my age
It's ten and seven I must engage

I feel much younger than that number
But it's time to think I will fumble
When colour dye is mentioned
I'll pretend it's a mere invention

CS: Don't think I would recognise you without your red hair Marie Louise!

DJ: Excellent poem. Reflects much how I feel at the moment.

PW: Dear Marie Louise, your poem very moving. Dear Roddy, brought your Supernatural Scotland out of quarantine. Surprised you could talk to a child ghost. If I ever saw such things always thought best to hide. I have some stories to share another time. After lockdown when we can all meet up again. A winter's night, roaring fires and stories, such stories.

Callum Stark

WHAT to do about contrast? You would think, this being the theme I set, it would be easiest for me to write. And yet, it has been the hardest. I feel and know that the subject is an important one – that's why I chose it; I feel and know that there is something profound and eloquent within me to say on the subject – this won't be it. No, instead I'll take shelter in the words of a sharper mind: the poet Atilla Josef. He wrote in his work The Seventh:

> **If you set out in the world**
> **better be born seven times.**
> **Once, in a house on fire,**
> **once in a freezing flood,**
> **once, in a wild madhouse,**
> **once in a field of ripe wheat,**
> **once in an empty cloister,**
> **and once among pigs in a sty.**
> **Six babies crying, not enough;**
> **you yourself must be the seventh.**

Words to live by; words I have tried to live by. Along with those of an elderly cowboy, who told me to seek out the most contrasting of situations: euphoric and despairing, highbrow and low, uncomfortable and cosy. For each will prise open your mind broad, Broader, Broadest.

As with Roddy's suburban naturist, I feel it's the contrast of life that keeps me going. I would never want to know only one type of person, or read only one type of book, or go to only one type of party for then I would only think one type of thing. To this end, I even have friends who are Tories.

Indeed, I remember clearly thinking it the oddest realisation, as a child, that we could change what we saw, felt and heard, but never that it was us doing the seeing, feeling or hearing. We have a permanent perspective, from within our own minds and bodies.

How easy it is to never waver from that perspective. Our very own bubble. Oh, how simple life could be if we all each stayed in our bubbles?

Well, many do – organising life so as to never see or meet anything or one of contrast to themselves. But more fool them because in my book, contrast is the only way to grow, to transcend in some small way these minds and bodies we're stuck with.

Barbara Dickson

THE best example of contrast I have popping into my mind is the Tai Chi symbol, the Yin and Yang two-toned circle with dots.

I remember in the 1970s seeing it everywhere as folks became more aware of diet and lifestyle, and stickers with this logo appeared in windows as a mission statement for the alternative option. In London, where I lived, we all became vegetarian. I remained a vegetarian for 25 years until the flatulence got the better of me.

This, in itself, was a huge contrast to the mince and tatties of my 1950s childhood, where we had enough, but not too much food, and very plain it was.

I sometimes can't believe how little we ate then and how healthy we were too.

I was just into my 30s when I attended classes at the City Lit. and everywhere was all Tai Chi and Yoga, American consciousness books by Sandra Ray and, of course, 'macrobiotic thinking', where one was encouraged to eat the food local to one's place of residence. No more pineapples!

My Keyboardist, Ian, came on tour once with a massive suitcase, packed by his then wife Brenda, containing all the things he might need to remain true to his macrobiotic diet. Jars, packets and potions galore, stuffed into a giant Globetrotter.

Brenda then ran away while Ian was on tour, with a massage therapist from Rayne's Park, who was, like her, obsessed with diet and lifestyle, unlike poor Ian, who was just henpecked!

Obviously, the liturgy of the enlightened didn't include kindness to husbands!

DJ: Very interesting and witty. Thanks Barbara. Brought a smile on a dreary day. X

CS: I can sympathise with your keyboardist Barbara, having a very health conscious mum. We almost always get stopped at airport security while my mum explains what this pulse or that grain or that powder is. Great piece x

PW: Thank you Dorothy, I'm there with Barbara, mince and tatties, bisto, spam, corned beef, stew with lentils, sometimes oats loads of veg added to spin out a pound of meat for 8... Did the veggie thing as well. Lockdown, lovely food delivered to me from a local farm. So, soup and stew... What goes round!

Dorothy Jackson

I spent 38 mostly happy years as a teacher at Lanark Grammar School. I remember the delight I felt when I heard that that was the school I had been allocated. In those days there was no such things as an interview and I am sure I got the position at Lanark because I had a car!

I was born and brought up in Wishaw, the better end of the burgh of Motherwell and Wishaw – or so my mother used to say. I was thrilled to learn that every day I would be driving from an urban area to a rural town.

I met another new teacher on the first day when the Headteacher suggested that she and I might like to travel together. I had a car, she didn't. Early on in our initiation into Lanark, we realised that Lanark had something like 22 feeder primary schools. Many of the children were bussed to school so it was decided that she and I would take a trip around the area to see where all these villages were.

Names such as Pettinain, Glespin, Kilncadzow, Ponfeigh, The Forth and The Junction (The use of 'The' preceding some of these villages was widely used by locals – I don't know why?)

The school had 1800 pupils and took in pupils from the local Catholic primary school as well. Ironically, Catholic pupils who wanted to attend a Catholic school had to travel by bus to Wishaw. I had come from a town with 4 secondary schools and apart from a few pupils from places such as Carluke and The Shotts, most of us walked to school.

Many of the Lanark pupils lived on farms or had parents who were farm workers and had quite a different outlook from the kids in the schools I had either been a pupil in, or a student teacher. In these schools many children were looking for apprenticeships in the steel or engineering works in Wishaw and Motherwell.

It was also easy to commute to Glasgow for higher education. In Lanark, many of the children were destined to work on farms or in some of the new businesses starting up in the industrial estate. Lanark was a designated enterprise zone in 1977 and businesses were being encouraged to move into the area with financial incentives.

This was partly because of rural deprivation through fewer jobs in the area as farms became more mechanised. Teachers were given council housing in order to entice them to the area. Even now, Lanark and Biggar can be looked on as 'out in the sticks.'

The children of Lanark were keen to find out all about their teachers. When they realised you were not from Lanark or its surrounding area, you were known as a 'doon througher'. Even if you only came from Carluke, 6 miles away.

I was such a person but I quickly embraced Lanark and its culture. The school is one of the oldest in Scotland and received its charter in 1183. The town is steeped in history and it had a castle and the Royal Mint. Wishaw High School, on the other hand, seemed to exist as a higher grade school only from 1906.

Lanark had an annual tradition called Lanimer Day (except this year, of course). Wishaw had a Co-op Gala Day. Although both involved children dressing up and there being a Queen, that is where the similarities ended. It's enough to cause a fight if one were to describe Lanimers as a Gala Day. Lanark has lorries in the procession – not floats, as was pointed out to me early on in my time in Lanark.

Lanark Grammar School regularly participated in Lanimers and it was a stressful time of highs and lows. Much work went into our contribution to the procession includ-ing the construction of some sort of feature around a moving vehicle. This could be a tractor or a trailer with adornment.

There would also be accompanying suitably dressed children and adults. One of the school's entries was a homage to the school show that year and was called 'The Dracula Spectacula'. There were a number of parts to this entry including Dracula's bride lying on a bed being looked over by Dracula.

Unfortunately, as the bed was being pushed down the High Street, one of the bed legs found a hole in the road and the bride was flung out of the bed onto the road. She was unharmed and quickly retook her position.

All who worked on an entry experienced the excitement and stress of perhaps having to stay up all night to get it finished. Then there was the absolute certainty that they would never do this again, only to agree after the event, to do it again the next year. Memories were short when it came to this.

Lanark has a market. Wishaw also had a market so no difference there except that Lanark's market is thriving and Wishaw's is no more. I remember early on in my career a pupil bringing a ferret into school that they had just bought at the market. It was kept in a box all day and then taken home on the school bus.

One of the things I loved about my job in Lanark was the journey to work. Over the 13 years that I commuted to Lanark, I had great company most of the time. In the sum-mer we would go home via The Valley and stop at one of the garden centres and pick strawberries; in autumn, we would buy plums and eat these on the way home.

I still love an urban environment where there are shops and cafes and a real buzz. I'm missing this during the lockdown but I'm very happy in my rural setting.

I miss going to Aviemore and seeing the mountains but I can still see some hills (no Munros but a Graham or two) from my daily walk around the graveyard. I have a clear view of Tinto Hill and have watched the small patch of snow retreat over these weeks of lockdown.

PW: Lovely contribution Dorothy. You were very lucky to find a job in a happy school. X

DJ: I was. X

RM: Thanks Dorothy. That was a really interesting read. I've always been attracted to Lanark. I can remember my mother taking us to look at Lauder Ha', Harry Lauder's house at Strathaven when I was a teenager. The last time I was in Lanark was last year for Catherine's aunt's memorial service.

DJ: Billy's grandmother's niece Anne Russell's son stayed at Lauder Ha'. They have the haulage firm Russell of Bathgate. They own Lauder Ha'. John G Russell was very kind and entertained us a number of times. I remember Irene (Billy's mum) buying flowers to take. When I saw the amount, I thought it was a bit excessive until I realised quite what Lauder Ha' was!! X

RM: My Mum once played the fiddle for Lauder at a party. We all grew up with those songs and my good friend Jamie MacDougall was hoping to revive Jimmy Logan's one man play about Lauder for the Edinburgh Festival this year but this is obviously not happening.

DJ: Would that be a relative of Kirsty Maxwell Stuart? She's involved in the Scotland's Garden Scheme and my friend opens his garden in the Lanark area. Obviously not this year! I saw Jimmy Logan on a number of occasions. He told a great story of visiting his sister Annie Ross and meeting many famous people. Shame about the play though. 🤞 for another time.

RM: It was Kirsty's memorial last year. A lovely woman and a friend of my family.

I knew Jimmy Logan quite well and he was very supportive of my career when I started at *Scottish Field*. I last saw him over in Fife when he was doing the Lauder play at the Byre Theatre. A kind and good man

PW: Hi Roddy posted a photo for you of Harry Lauder just now on Facebook. If you like please share with *Decameron*, don't know how to do that.

DJ: I should have remembered she'd died. I 'm sorry. I'm sure my friend told me. It's such a shame the Scotland's Gardens won't be open this year as my friend has been using this time to work on his property. 🤞

CMS: Fascinating memories Dorothy- aspects of Peebles High without the ferrets and much more Catholic. I was amazed by the huge Catholic Church for Kirsty's memorial even though she wasn't a Catholic. Definitely know you're in the West!

DJ: St Mary's is a magnificent building. Refurbishment has made it a cosier place. My mother and aunt had slates purchased in their memory by my friend. Father Brannigan who sadly died when only about 58 was instrumental in its refurbishment. I was there recently and as usual was really impressed by it.

DJ: That's a fabulous photo of Harry Lauder. X

PW: Happy for you to share this. My grandfather at the back row right next to the cross. Harry Lauder is with Scottish Horse, served Gallipoli 1915. My understanding is very few of these Perthshire soldiers survived Gallipoli.

RM: The following year, Lauder's son, who was in the Argyll & Sutherland Highlanders, was killed by a sniper at the Battle of the Somme. Hence the story of Lauder going on stage after the telegram arrived and singing *Keep Right On To The End Of The Road*.

Jonathan Gibbs

Contrasting speeds of travel in the Animal Kingdom.

CONTRAST: Men & women-related true story: Mary Lacy was a poor Kentish girl who ran away from home in 1773 to escape from a lifetime as a domestic servant. She disguised herself as a man and joined the British Navy as an apprentice shipwright.

On being discovered, Mary Lacy was expelled so instead became an architect and builder of what is now Deptford High Street. She was the first woman to be given a British Admiralty pension.

Illustration: DEPTFORD WIVES commissioned for Radio Times.

INSIDE & OUTSIDE: a view from the window is framed by shutters. These are designed to keep out light and the heat of the sun.

However, slices of light penetrate between the slats. A wood-engraved block depends entirely upon those parts of the surface that remain intact, flat & smooth, to receive the ink, as opposed to the incised marks that are below this surface which receive no ink.

This is a process of subtraction; a process that employs absence. The white is the paper itself, the black is the sticky ink.

SHUTTERS exhibited Curwen Gallery, London.

RM: Brilliant Johnnie

MLM: Johnnie adore all your work and thanks for historic info too♥♫▶🔍🔍👍

CMS: Great contribution Johnnie. Just reading *Trumpet* by Jackie Kay based on a woman who disguised herself as a man so she could pursue her career as a jazz musician. And great contrast to that piece Callum – yes, contrast is quite a theme – thank goodness for the extension!

Andrew Brown

CHIAROSCURO is an aristic term derived from the Italian words for light and dark. It originated in the Renaissance from the practice of drawing figures on coloured paper using sepia ink for the darks and white gouache for the highlights but broadened in meaning later to cover all drawings and paintings with strong contrasts in illumination most dramatically exemplified in the work of Caravaggio and Rembrandt.

However, my inspiration and a more subtle exponent of the technique was the Spanish painter Velaszquez whose only nude is The Rokeby Venus now in the National Gallery in London, and painted around 1750 on his visit to Italy where he was influenced by the antique marble Borghese hermaphrodite as well as the female nudes of Titian.

My watercolour finished last night in the nick of time contributes to the present theme and borrows Velasquez's chiaroscuro trick of contrasting the pearly naked buttocks against the silky dark coverlet spread over the snowy sheets. I have also employed the so-called Venus effect showing the model's reflection in a mirror which is, of course, physically impossible since we see the face reflected in our direction.

Velasquez's masterpiece was slashed in 1914 by an irate suffragette in protest at the objectification of women by male chauvinists. However, I trust I can dodge such criticism since my model is a man.

DJ: Excellent Andrew! Glad you're painting. X

MLM: Love it great Andrew you're painting example is same painting shown and inspiring this week on life drawing on BBC.

MLM: But perfect your interpretation!!!

AB: What a coincidence Marie-Louise I had no idea BBC were doing life drawing but anyway I have just now finished this landscape from the terrace at Glen. I was attempting a chiaroscuro effect with the Scots pines against the sky but it clouded over a little so turned out rather romantic and Turneresque.

Catherine Maxwell Stuart

MY first school was in the rural idyll of Traquair Village presided over by the fearsome headmistress, Mrs Fiabane, who had all 25 of her pupils (aged 5-11) sitting at their desks in front of her. She would rap our fingers with a long wooden ruler for the slightest misdemeanour.

The upside was a woodland for a playground and nature walks across the Minch Moor where we would go off for a day with our pack lunches.

When winter came my mother decided that she missed London and we all moved down to live in my grandmother's house just opposite Harrods in Brompton Square. I loathed being in the city and my next school, Faulkner House, was a smart private school where the uniform consisted of blue tweed coats with red 'jelly bag hats' – knitted red horrors with a tassel on the end that reached half way down your back. No doubt so that the Chelsea mothers could coo at their sweet offspring.

The contrast could not have been more marked. Play time was in a concrete yard and for all the supposed privilege of those city children, my village school seemed infinitely superior.

Then it was back to Traquair in the summer, and the following winter it was back to another posh London school with some other strange uniform and a new set of friends. I became quite adept at being the new girl.

I was about 8 when my mother decided to buy a flat in Edinburgh and I was sent to St George's School for Girls. It was a school that seemed to pride itself on having the most ludicrous number of rules. Discipline was enforced through disorder marks, posted up weekly on the notice boards to shame the guilty, and three, which meant a visit to the headmistress was treated as worse than death.

There was an equal passion for uniform with instructions about the exact length of skirt down to the heavy duty nylon navy pants. We were made to do things like play tennis for an entire term without a ball (perfecting our strokes) and I was constantly petrified of unwittingly breaking a rule and getting a disorder mark.

The girls were cliquey. I had a love/hate relationship with one girl who was my "best friend." One week she would ignore me, the next she wouldn't leave me alone.

I loathed the school and everything about it. I set about persuading my mother to send me to a local school which took some time as she was overcoming her guilt at not having sent me to a convent boarding school, which was usually hurled at me as a final threat.

I won out eventually with a small compromise. I went to the Catholic Primary School in Peebles which had an enforced attendance at Mass once a week, weekly confession, morning prayers and a creepy priest. Suddenly there was no uniform except a grey skirt and tie – what joy!

The kids were normal and lived more in fear of bullies than teachers. There were some famously rough families: my friend Eddie Temple had lost an eye when he was five in a cocktail stick accident. On a visit to Peebles High School, he was hauled into the toilets by some bigger boys and we didn't see him again until he reappeared as we were about to leave looking a bit the worse for wear.

I ended up going to the High School for four years (my longest school experience). A real comprehensive school with such a good reputation, it attracted middle class families to move from Edinburgh but it was also a melting pot of different classes, experiences and behaviour. The only thing that would mark you out for real bullying or being accused of being "posh" was an English accent. This included the poor new boy who arrived from Lancashire.

Somehow I got away with affecting a little more Scottish at school than at home and survived unscathed. I finally left when I was 16 for a college in Edinburgh to get A levels.

In the end my school experience did give me a real insight into private v. state schools, single sex v. mixed, rural v. city life, but I left having no great love for any of them although perhaps a lingering nostalgia for those early nature walks over the hills at Traquair.

DJ: Great piece Catherine. So interesting. X

DS: Wonderful Catherine - the perfect exploration of contrast. Also I know all too well that St George's is such a disturbing school!

CS: Even now!

RM: Give me a girl at an impressionable age... xx

Mark Muller Stuart – Contrasts

SO, when I was asked to think of contrasts, my mind conjured up simultaneous images of three places that celebrate the splendour of human diversity and ingenuity but also our capacity for exclusion and to construct walls of contrasting division. The first was of Instanbul in 1993. The second of Palestine in 2008, and the third of Thomas Jefferson's home Monticello in 2013.

Turkey 1993

TO my mind there, can be no greater expression of the cultural diversity of human society than the city of Instanbul. I had the opportunity to explore its environs many times while teaching in Cyprus. But in 1993, I returned in another guise as a young human rights lawyer and trial observer. The Turkish Government had just instituted proceedings against a young female editor called Gurbetteli Orsov who ran *Ozgur Gundem*, a Kurdish newspaper and I had been asked to observe the trial for Article 19 after Arthur Miller and Harold Pinter wrote a petition in defence of its freedom of expression.

It soon became clear that the case was part of a wider attempt of the Turkish Government to crackdown on Kurdish culture and the campaign for greater Kurdish rights. It seems ludicrous from today's perspective but back then, the Turkish State was literally intent on denying and suppressing all form of expression of culture, including its so-called dialects, names, dances, songs and poems.

I soon discovered that beyond the prosecution, 22 journalists from the paper had gone missing, which in turn led me to the killing fields of south-east Turkey where 3 million Kurds were being forcibly displaced. Some of the journalists' bullet-ridden bodies were found on its lonely roadsides from where they had been reporting.

I can still recall returning back to Istanbul and walking around the beautiful avenues around the Topkapi Palace near where the trial was being held and trying to grasp how the same city could house such completely different political realities. The experience would lead me to establish the Kurdish Human Rights Project, which would bring over 400 cases against the Turkish Government in the European Court of Human Rights for failures to protect the right to contrast.

But if I'm honest, it is not the legal submissions made or the eloquent judgements handed down by the great and the good in the courtrooms of Strasbourg that I remember now. No, what is burnt into my memory is hearing the news that our first applicant was shot dead by the authorities; witnessing my Kurdish driver being forced to kneel down as an automatic rifle was placed in his mouth by soldiers in search of information at a desolate checkpoint; seeing a military colonel drive over a small Kurdish boy without so much as a look back; meeting twelve-year old paper boys who had their arms cut off for selling opposition papers; recalling the utter fear of our legal colleagues in Diyarbakir in 1994, who refused to even look at me as they were dragged into the dock of the Turkish State Security Courts, after enduring days of gruesome detention for merely filing human rights claims to the European Court; and later on, the images of the decapitated corpse of Ersöz who was mutilated by Turkish special forces after signing up with the Kurdish equivalent of the Red Crescent.

These are the images of contrast that I retain in my mind's eye. They have a photographic quality about them. But there are other less haunting images.

I cannot forget the simple but gracious hospitality of the Kurdish villagers I came across after their isolated and poverty-stricken homes had been burnt by the Turkish military in the summer of 1994. They had just lost some of their young menfolk, who were run over by a passing tank, and were awaiting others who had fled to hide in the fields.

Yet as dusk fell and their loved ones returned, it was we, not they, who were fed with what meagre rations they had left. "Tell the world what is happening here," one said, "It is a miracle you have come," said another.

These first-hand experiences change one's perspective about law, conflict and the protection of human rights. They bind you to a region and people in ways that are scarcely imaginable to you at the outset.

I remember meeting some dissident journalists in the back streets of Sultan Ahmet in old Istanbul in November 1994, for a late-night meal, after they had got the morning edition out. We had just missed the bombing of *Ozgur Gundem*'s building by some thirty minutes. All my companions chain-smoked and looked nervously at the door as they ate, conscious that the knock on the door and the midnight run to the security cell could happen at any time.

But what I also recall was the laughter, the stolen glances of tenderness between them. There was a collective recognition that they should live in the moment, as any of their number may not be dining with them the following night.

In a strange and very real sense, they all seemed so totally alive. They were caught up in a history of their own making. They felt proud to be involved in the fight to convey their version of the truth which, in a normal, pluralist society, would have been permitted.

Mark in South-East Turkey documenting the destruction of Kurdish villages and homes with Channel 4 News.

The Enduring Middle East 2008

THE second group of images are from Palestine. Contrasts made me think of a series of trips I made to the Middle East between 2006-10 with Andrew, Catherine and Delfina Entrecanales while we set up the Delfina Foundation and I wrote a book with Scottish landscape artist Joseph Maxwell Stuart entitled *The Enduring Middle East: In the Footsteps of David Roberts* (2012).

Joseph and I traversed the Middle East to retrace the steps of the Scottish artist David Roberts, who captured the Holy Land, Egypt and Nubia in over 300 iconic lithographs between 1838 and 1842. His images framed much of the West's vision of the Middle East in the nineteenth century. We wanted to see whether the landscapes of Roberts had survived the ravages of the twentieth century.

The contrasts between then and now were many. In embarking on the project, I was conscious that Robert's lithographs sat uneasily with the modern realities of the Middle East.

To many, the Middle East was a place of unending conflict, where dysfunctional governments, rampant unchecked growth, torture and brutality reigned supreme. For them the landscapes of Roberts were irrevocably scarred by the pillbox, minefield, refugee camps, but above all, by border checkpoints and invidious security walls behind which communities that had once lived side by side in relative peace were now separated by fear and loathing. What relevance did Robert's Victorian images have for us today? Were his lithographs just a stylised glimpse of a largely idealised bygone age or were they indicative of a more enduring culture that still informed the Middle East and its people?

Yet it was fascinating to lose oneself in the mists of time, whether at Saqqara, Giza, or in the Sinai Desert. I remember being entranced by the sheer history and architectural splendour of the Middle East as toured Baalbek in Lebanon, Palmyra in Syria, and Petra in Jordan. Together we came across unvarnished places like Sebastia near Nablus in Palestine, where we encountered lost Roman ruins with vistas of breathtaking splendour, diminished only by the network of twenty first century Israeli checkpoints that had sliced up the blanket of ancient rolling Palestinian hilltop villages.

As Joseph and I traversed across Egypt, the Sinai and Jordan, it became clear that much of the old Middle East remained intact beyond its ancient monuments. Whether among the Felucca boatmen in Aswan, the teeming crowds in old Cairo, or the ever-hospitable Bedouin of Wadi Rum, it was still possible to immerse oneself in the timeless ways of the past. A sense of historical perpetuity often pervades ancient sites, but this can be a deeply deceptive sentiment. Change can come quickly and brutally in the Middle East and when it does, it is no respecter of diversity or antiquity.

Perhaps the most disturbing example of such change that we came across was in the ancient city of Hebron in occupied Palestine, where the tomb of Abraham is to be found. Hebron had for centuries been home to a multitude of Palestinians and one of the oldest Jewish communities. Roberts records on the 17th March 1893 that there were 1,300 families, four of which were Jewish, and one Christian.

These communities co-existed side by side for centuries until, that is, the state of Israel was created. Now the ancient centre of the city has been taken over by Jewish settlers with the assistance of 4,000 Israeli soldiers who patrol its quarters. These settlers pour out burning oil and rubbish from their high-rise homes onto the few remaining Palestinians who are permitted to work in the darkened alleyways below. It is deeply disturbing to walk through this once thriving city with soldiers on every rooftop with their protective nets hanging ominously above.

The ritual humiliation meted out to the Palestinians who, in order to get into the old city or visit the Mosque of Abraham, are routinely required to queue in the beating hot sun for hours at threatening checkpoints as settlers leisurely amble past unrestricted, remains deeply troubling.

Today, the age-old traditional hospitality that previously characterised this place, as grand caravansaries of pilgrims made their way to worship together at the collective hilltop shrine of Abraham's Tomb, venerated by all three great religions of the world, has been lost to a world of barbed-wire contrast.

The tomb is now cordoned off for Jews after a right-wing settler mowed down 29 Muslim pilgrims in 1994 and the authorities took the opportunity to impose its own form of securitised black-and-white contrast on what had otherwise been a symbol of human cultural diversity.

The experience helped teach me that the drivers of all conflicts are based upon one form of exclusion or another and that no society can be at peace with itself unless it either agrees to or confronts the contrasts it imposes on itself.

Monticello 2013

THIS leads me to my third set of images from the house of Thomas Jefferson, author of the 1776 Declaration of American Independence, who wrote that all men are created equal by their creator who endowed them with certain unalienable rights.

Monticello is a beautiful house full of the most delightful artefacts from the world of science and art. Jefferson spent many months here designing aspects of the building in the French and Italian styles, and writing correspondence to John Adams with one eye on his reputation which, revealingly on his deathbed, he asked James Madison to protect after he had gone.

I can still recall the delight in coming across a similar Harpsichord to the one at Traquair, which originally belonged to the 6th Earl of Traquair's eldest daughter, Christian Stuart who, in 1770, eloped with an American law student studying at Edinburgh University called Cyrus Griffin, for the wilds of revolutionary America. Yet that delight soon turned to horror as I looked out of the window towards the slave-quarters that lined the avenue leading up to the house, where Jefferson secretly housed his other black family.

His white daughter would play her instrument inside while he sold the offspring of his other black family to his white relatives. The contrast between the words of the Declaration of Independence and the sordid truth behind the beautiful facade on Monticello has only slowly revealed itself over the decades.

The truth is Jefferson was born into one of the richest families in Virginia but died owing 2 million dollars and with hundreds of slaves whom he failed to free in this lifetime. Cyrus, on the other hand, would become the 10th President of the Continental Congress and a Federal Court Judge in Virginia, where he would sit on a series of cases with John Marshall, whose verdicts invoked the wrath of a vengeful Jefferson as they built a constitutional edifice based upon national government and the rule of law.

Cyrus would quietly sit on that bench for another twenty years and die leaving in his Will an instruction that he be buried unmarked for the least possible expense next to his beloved wife, Christina, in Bruton Church, Williamsburg.

I know which grave I would rather be next to for despite all of Jefferson's fine words and public accolades one gets the impression – as one takes in the full history of the contrasts of that shining house upon the hill- that he died alone by himself without his slave mistress beside him or a redeeming conscience to console his troubled and divided mind.

RM: Impressive Mark. A powerful indictment of the futility of cruelty.

AB: I remember the barbed unpleasantness of Hebron as well as the desolate grandeur of Palmyra and the kindness of everyone we met in Syria and Palestine

By the way Pat has asked me to let everyone know that the next theme from tomorrow in tribute to Roddy's book is The Supernatural

BD: Excellent and most thought provoking, Mark. Thank you.

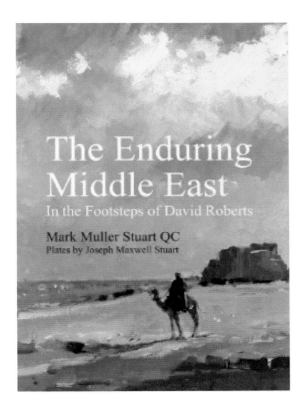

Jessie Ann Matthew

TIME TO GO

TULIPS

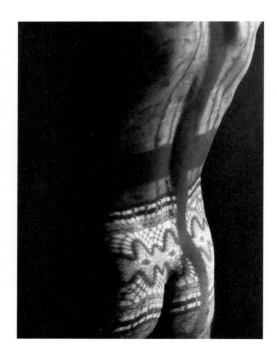

CONTRAST

SUPERNATURAL

Roddy Martine

I have genuinely never understood why anyone should be scared of the supernatural. I have only ever thought of the presence of ghosts from a hypothetical afterlife as reassuring; I rather like the idea of being watched over lovingly, although perhaps not all of the time.

Once you accept ghosts exist, you can also assume they are all around us. Some might even be your relatives, benign, inquisitive and, I like to think, protective.

As souls caught between assumed metaphysical spheres of existence, they mean us no harm. I've also never understood why organised western religions which are largely based on the supernatural, are so hostile towards the subject.

Yes, of course there are poltergeists bent on mischief. But if you venture deep enough into their history and that of their surroundings, there is always an explanation.

I discovered this when researching my books "*Supernatural Scotland*" (Robert Hale: 2003) and "*Haunted Scotland*" (Birlinn:2010). From childhood, I have, in all innocence, heard, seen, sensed and experienced any amount of strange aberrations (while sober) which I have been unable to rationally explain.

Manifestations do not perform to order. You can spend endless nights in medieval dungeons anticipating temperatures to rise and drop, which they usually do.

Yet it would seem ghosts only materialise when they choose to and the majority of us are conditioned not to notice. Only small children see the funny old woman who sits under a tree in the park feeding the unicorn.

At Castle Menzies in Perthshire, I encountered an elegant lady with a child whom I later discovered could not possibly have been there.

At a remote cottage on Loch Hourne in Wester Ross, I too heard the approaching tramp of marching feet in the dead of night, an experience shared with the writer Gavin Maxwell.

Exploring the Goblin Ha' under croft of Yester Castle in the Lammermuirs, I was physically pushed out of a subterranean passage by some unseen malignant force. I have seen the green men rise out of the waves of the Sound of Shiant in the Hebrides. Staying overnight in the Duke's Bedroom at Ackergill Tower in Caithness, I witnessed the shadow of Helen Gunn of Braemore as she threw herself from the battlements in 1450.

"Once you eliminate the impossible, whatever remains, no matter how improbable, has to be the truth," wrote Sir Arthur Conan Doyle.

Although himself caught up in a comical hoax over the existence of fairies, the words he attributed to Sherlock Holmes make absolute sense to me.

During my research I came across medians and seers and druids, white witches and fortune tellers. Such is the cynicism of our times that many of those who confided in me begged not to be named, terrified of what others might think. Yet behind closed doors I discovered that at least three out of five had a story to tell.

I was naturally nervous when invited to speak to the Edinburgh College of Parapsychology but my audience could not have been more welcoming and understanding. They knew what I was talking about and they even asked me back again the following year.

One of the stories in Haunted Scotland concerns two young cyclists from Glasgow being stalked by a phantom panther through the Galloway Forest Park. Having been summoned to talk at the Wigtown Book Festival, I set off and entirely by accident missed the A75 junction. This meant I unintentionally found myself driving through the Galloway Forest Park, a rather longer route than anticipated.

Familiar road signs popped up - Glen Trool, Clatteringshaws Loch and the Black Loch.

As I accelerated, the sky grew darker and the rain became relentless. Spectacular scenery loomed up on all sides. There appeared to be nobody else on the lonely road until I came across a BMW which had been driven into a ditch. I offered the driver, shaken but unhurt, a lift to the nearest civilisation. "It was a large black cat," he told me. "It ran straight across the road in front of me. I slammed on my brakes. It nearly killed me!"

Then there was the grand dame A.J. Stewart who lived on the fourth floor of a tenement in St Vincent Street in Edinburgh who was convinced that she was the reincarnation of James IV, King of Scots.

Having died violently on the battlefield of Flodden in 1513, she was back to see Scotland become independent again."When you have a horrible death accompanied by desperate feelings of guilt and anger and frustration, of course you want to come back to finish the job," she told me.

My favourite anecdote is of Gordon McNeill-Wilkie, a Perthshire medium, who had been called upon to exorcise Ashentully Castle at Blairgowrie. Having, as he thought, done so, he discovered that three black hooded old women had travelled home with him in his car.

All of us are simply passing through time. Science admits time can be reversed albeit to date only minimally. If we can send men to the stars, why shouldn't we re-visit the past? Why shouldn't the past visit us? It's all about space and time and elecricity, it would seem.

Until the world of the supernatural is satisfactorily explained, the most important thing for all of us to remember is to keep an open mind. No matter how improbable anything might appear to be, what remains has to be believed.

CS: A tough act to follow Roddy!

BD: Excellent, Roddy. I love this! Bx

RM: xxx Barbara

CMS: Brilliant Roddy! I remember AJ Stewart coming to Traquair and insisting she had spent the night here in her previous incarnation. We all thought her crazy but who knows?

RM: God Bless her! I am told she is now in a home competing with her late mother who lived to be 100! Hope she's survives the virus. x

PW: Thank you Barbara and Roddy. Is the story of Charlie Robertson of Canongate Kirk in one of your books Roddy?

RM: Yes. in Chapter 16 of Supernatural Scotland although rather more chilling than your gentle experience. Charlie was the only clergyman (Church of Scotland) who would talk to.me about exorcism.

PW: I get that Roddy absolutely, have other stories... Look forward to sharing some day when all of this is past. Not for writing down... I'm at chapter 11 of Supernatural Scotland, Will fast forward. Thank you

PW: Remind me Rev IM Wright?

RM: Rev Charlie Robertson was the Queen' s Chaplain at Canongate Kirk but the story concerned him when he was a young man up north. He is still going strong taking services at St Cuthbert's in the West End.

Somebody once very kindly advised, "don't read alone ...!"

PW: I'll be okay Roddy, been just appreciating this conversation with us all. And besides we are never entirely alone. Warning noted though. Hoping to hear from Moira currently on the move from Texas to Michigan.

Callum Stark

THESE drawings – done very quickly – have all in some way to do with ghosts. The first: I've always felt that the biggest privilege is to share food with others, a difficult task in lockdown!

Though on occasion when I eat lunch alone at the table or occasionally dinner without my family, I do not really feel alone; I see the memories – 'ghosts' – of all those who would normally be round the table breaking bread. I'm comforted by these memories of feasts gone by just as I am comforted by the thought of genuine ghosts living among us.

I've often wondered too, whether ghosts adhere to the same structures of life as the living – do they rush off thinking they must not be late for dinner and pull up an empty chair?

The second set of drawings were done at the same time racking my brain for supernatural material, I have begun to draw in pastel again for the first time in a long time.

Flicking through my scribblings I had forgotten how pastel can rub against the opposite page and render your drawing a ghostly blur. In tandem, as we begin to leave lockdown, I've been thinking introspectively about these aspects of my personality that have faded away in the absence of people – being quite a sociable person.

As such, I did two amateurish self-portraits: the left is me, in my whole state; the second, fading away.

CS: + As I ran out of paper in my big sketchbook, if you look very carefully you can see the ghost of a drawing of a man in his 70s called Alastair, nude save only for a parasol, which I had to rub out to accommodate this drawing!

RM: Great drawings Callum. I should imagine that Andrew is probably in the Tweed as we write. Happy to Zoom later or on Tuesday.

MMS: Catherine and I are heading for the Tweed as we text. Will look out for the lesser spotted Brown

RM: And the pilot fish?

Mark Muller Stuart – Supernatural

WHEN I was asked by Decameron to dwell on events or things that cannot be explained by nature or science and that are assumed to come from beyond or to originate from otherworldly forces, three instances in my own life came to mind. To this day, I have been unable to account for their occurrence.

The first occurred when I was around eleven and travelling back from our family's home in the Black Forest in Baden-Wurttemberg to catch a ferry to Boulogne. As a young boy I, like many of my age, was captivated by WWII. Not only did I lose three great uncles at Stalingrad, another uncle was held captive by the Soviets until 1952.

While my grandfather on my father's side fought for the Allies at Monte Casino, and on my mother's side deserted the German Army and walked back from Yugoslavia, finally being rescued from a hospital in Prague by his wife.

As a boy, I eagerly read comics like Warlord, marvelling at the antics of the commandos. I became an expert in deciphers. I also developed a quiet fascination for Dunkirk.

But that was nothing as to the sheer force that took hold of me as we raced to catch the ferry to Boulogne when I suddenly, and unaccountably, told my mother we had to turn off the main road.

She looked at me as if I was mad. "We only have an hour or so to catch the ferry," she remonstrated.

But I had become all but hysterical and so she relented.

"Turn left," I shouted. "Now right," and so it went on as I proceeded to direct her out of instinct to a place just outside of Dunkirk.

Suddenly the houses gave way to tufts of sandy grass reliefs. "Stop!" I shouted.

We all got out of the car as I proceeded to ramble up and down the dunes until I came to an unnatural mound of grass set back 400 yards from the beach.

"There," I pointed.

"Where?" asked my sister.

"In there," I retorted, pointing to the mound. "I've been here before," and with that we moved around the mound to discover a concrete opening into an overgrown bunker and battery.

My mother looked at me in astonishment. We went inside, It was clearly a place where soldiers had made a last stand to keep the Germans from overrunning the beach.

"Satisfied?" asked my mother, and with that we turned and ran back to the car in a desperate attempt to get to the ferry.

To this day, I'm not sure whether all of this happened due to a furtive imagination and some sense that we were near Dunkirk or because of something more elemental. I don't believe in reincarnation but the sense of having been there before was overwhelming.

The second instance occurred in May of 1983. In the same week as my father died, his second wife's father also passed away. As we prepared for the funeral, I had a dream in which my father appeared. He was worried because he wanted to pay back somebody called 'Tony' the 20 pounds he owed him.

I knew of no Tony that was a friend of his or associated with him, so thought no more of it.

However, I did tell his Irish wife, Leo, who had to go to Ireland to attend her father's funeral. When she came back to England, she told me the oddest thing.

After she had buried her father, she went to the Wake where she talked to the priest. She realised suddenly that his name was Tony, so she asked him whether my father had ever borrowed money from him.

"Come to think of it, he did," replied the priest. "He owed me £20 pounds. I gave it to him one time when he needed money for a Taxi."

The third instance occurred three months of so later. I was staying with a girlfriend when at about 2am in the morning I awoke, sat bolt upright, turned to her and said, "I need to call my mother. She is in danger."

"What?" replied my girlfriend, somewhat dumbfounded.

Again, some uncontrollable force seemed to take hold of me. So I called my Mother who was living with her partner Graham in Chalfont St Giles in Buckinghamshire.

They lived in the country in a 16th century house that was once owned by Lord Cokes. "You are in danger," I told her. "Don't know why, but you are."

My mother proceeded to convince me she was perfectly fine, so we all went back to bed.

About an hour later, my mother and Graham heard banging on one of the doors leading to the patio inside the walled garden. They crept down to find a woman in her nighty crying out,"help me!"

They opened the door whereupon the young woman proceeded to tell them that she lived in one of the houses over the hill and that a mad woman had just attacked her in the middle of the night. She had fled but her young son was left in the house.

My mother and Graham put on their clothes and scrambled over the fields towards the old house. As they got to the gravel pathway, they saw that the door was wide open, and that a light was on in the hallway.

They approached the entrance but then were met with the vision of a small boy with just his pyjama top on, holding his penis peeing on the floor seemingly singing to himself but clearly in shock.

My mother rushed towards him. As she entered the house, she was attacked by what she later said was a witch-like thing who leapt onto her back, grabbed hold of her hair and began to dig her nails deep into her skin.

Graham immediately came to the rescue and my mother struggled free, bruised and bleeding. Graham then proceeded to wrestle to the floor a bewitched woman of inordinate strength. The tussle went on for almost a minute before he finally managed to pin her to the floor with her entreating him to 'fuck' her.

Luckily, within a few minutes the police came and took her away. It later emerged that this woman had been sectioned and had escaped from a local mental hospital. However, no one really understood exactly what and why the incident had occurred.

I cannot account for what made me sit bolt upright that night although I have always had a heightened sense of protection towards my family. I am not a believer or purveyor of grand theories about the supernatural.

Nor have I ever sought to ridicule those who sense an existence of something beyond our five senses. I just live in the world as I find it.

Not everything has to be explicable for it to be real to me. But neither does the inexplicable detain me. There are enough examples of parallel universes in our own human discourse and interactions to at least entertain the thought that other unmapped phenomena might perhaps exist, be they in nature or in our extraordinary and often uncontrolled imagination and sense of connection to elements beyond our immediate understanding.

It would appear that some of the cracks between these parallel universes might just have opened up for a short while in these three instances in a life lived in an otherwise worldly terrain.

DJ: So interesting Mark.

RM: Are you per chance a seventh child? I know that sounds a bit cliched, but my mother was the seventh child of a seventh child and I grew up with her premonitions, all regarding family. She was always proved correct. When my sister fell off her scooter in Marble Arch she knew about it before the hospital telephoned her, and turned back home from taking me to the cinema (much to my annoyance!)

As for Dunkirk I think all of us at one time or another have been somewhere they know they have been before but can't explain where or when. Something to do with the psyche and the volume of energy absorbed by the surroundings. Perhaps best not to be too analytical.

MMS: Thanks Roddy and Dorothy and apologies for typos in my script as I was rushing it out to try to enjoy the weather. Alas I'm not in 7th heaven. Are we doing a Zoom this evening?

Marie-Louise Brulatour Mills

I touched it as if it were electric pulling my finger away quickly. I didn't understand why I did that. It made no sense. After all it was a mere inanimate object, a small stone. Why was I afraid of it?

I stood there looking into a shoe-box of bric-a-brac, things long forgotten but cherished in some way. It was next to a small broken doll, a chipped porcelain one the size of a thumb. I imagined a young child dressing it, pulling small trousers on its flexible legs and a jacket while turning its bendable shoulders. My old friend Michelle gave it to me but I couldn't remember why. I never liked it or even played with dolls. I placed it back in the junk box.

Staring at the box of miscellaneous objects I returned to that small stone, picked it up fearlessly now and sat down on the winged chair to study it. Stripes of strong sunlight slashed through its lamp black colour, allowing a faint deep coppery shade to shine through it. I gazed at it as I circulated one finger over its smooth surface as if I had an Aladdin's lamp, soon images appeared.

As I continued to feel its smooth source and rounded edges I returned to them, when I was 18 years old sitting on a rock jutting up from the sea near my host's home in Tobermory on the Isle of Mull. I was a debutante then doing the Grand Tour with two English women as chaperones and another dozen girls from America's Eastern seaboard.

Mrs Righton, the shorter of the two spinster chaperones had some distant cousins on Mull, so Tobermory ranked with Rome, Paris, London, Edinburgh, Florence, Brussels, on our itinerary.

We stayed in a cross between a manor house and a farmhouse as the ponies, dogs, sheep were all around. The family, named Forrester, were kind, gentle, generous with explanations and so the environment was not merely comfortable and welcoming, but refreshing away from any hotel.

They had four children, two boys slightly older than any of us. Most of the girls in the group were boy crazy so for them they made concerted efforts to befriend the boys.

I, on the other hand, was a champion equestrian and a bookworm, which left little time for this game. I would spend some of the day patting the animals, sketching them and making friends with the four legged creatures so near.

One day, I wandered down to the water. I was just gazing into the distance and throwing an occasional rock out to the sea but was abruptly stopped by a voice from behind, and there began a life long adventure.

The images of sixty years ago were as fresh as the cool waters that slipped through my fingers when we waved our hands into it. This slow, silent and steady action accompanied our conversations about dreams, poetry and life generally. I would read his palm turning over his long artistic fingers to find fewer lines than mine as we compared them.

The second day we walked along a path and Robin pointed out a simple house cascading into a ruin, pieces of wood, perhaps a stairway crumbled to its stone floor and frame-less windows exposed their cracked and smashed selves.

"This is it," he said as we stopped. He told me about a Minister who lived here that preached about the Clearances as it if was a good and noble creed. One day after preaching, and a quiet lunch in the Manse, he dozed off on his chair.

When he awoke, the house was shrouded in darkness and, searching for candles, he stumbled and fell to the ground. He claimed later a crofter appeared with a pitchfork and did so every night until one evening he screamed and his pierced body fell to the floor, and while bloodless, he died. Some say he was the work of the devil by his screeching preaching and goodness had been drained from him long ago.

"Robin, are there more stories?" I asked.

"Yes," he said those sixty years ago.

We communicated via transatlantic Christmas cards for years. One year, I didn't receive one and wrote to him and, as it was unanswered, wrote again. I had been moving and address changes never quite caught up with me in Italy.

I received a reply finally and opened it with excitement to hear his current news but it was very short and from his brother.

Robin married an Irish woman painter and, as you know, he was a painter. They divorced and he took his own life," wrote his brother.

I crumpled up the letter, wept and wondered if those short lines on his palm meant this all along. His lifeline stopped mid-way through, but when I go there now in my memory he appears to me at night often showing me a painting as we walk hand-in-hand to the water's edge.

PW: Oh Marie Louise, so beautifully written. Your story and Barbara's singing reduced me to tears, so lovely. Thank youX

RM: Lost love across the years. I'm sure Robin is waiting for you on the shore, Marie Louise. I have to drive up to Mull to do a write up on Duart when all of this lockdown is over so perhaps, we could go and have a look?

MLM: Thank you. Hard to write a bit blinded by my emotion. Loved Barbara's song and Johnnys great work and Callum's sketches. Thanks Roddy needed a wee boost and yes love to revisit xxxx

Dorothy Jackson

'THE concept of the supernatural encompasses all entities, places and events that supposedly fall outside the scope of scientific understanding of the laws of nature' – so states Wikipedia!

When I read this definition I realise how wide ranging this is.

I was discussing the topic with my son Andrew who has a science background and when I mentioned the above quote, he was quite entertained by it. He remembered when he was young being obsessed with the supernatural. Encouraged by my aunt!

He chose books about conspiracy theories, the paranormal and the occult. I suppose I encouraged him in this by buying these books. He says he's still a fan of the supernatural and the feelings that these stories evoke. I am a great Harry Potter fan and that's about as scary as I can cope with. I have over the last few years dipped into Stephen King books. The ones I have read are crime and only have a smidgen of supernatural. No horror for me. Just a nice murder.

I was once photographed by Stephen King whilst having a meal in rural Maine. I couldn't believe it as I am a big fan!

I have never had a supernatural experience. Although, I do remember an incident whilst on holiday in Dublin with my friend. We decided to visit Malahide Castle as we had done the usual tourist stuff in Dublin and when consulting the guide book we thought it sounded interesting.

We got there and decided to take the tour of the castle. Things were going well and we were impressed and interested. We went into a few rooms and then on entering the third room, my friend stopped and said that she had a funny feeling about the room and, in fact, didn't feel well.

I suggested that we go to the coffee shop in the castle and give her time to recover. We got there and sat down with our coffee and scones and she suddenly announced that she felt fine!

She had not had a feeling of deja vu but she had just remembered that she had visited the castle before. So much for the ghost in the room!

CS: Wonderful Dorothy - did you notice Stephen King at the time or only afterwards?

DJ: I admit I contrived the photo to have him in it. My son was very impressed.

RM: Great Dorothy. Doesn't the ghost of the beautiful Maud Plunkett run around Malahide looking for her third husband? I was told this by one of her descendants.

DJ: Interesting. I will research this Roddy. They say there's a ghost in the hotel at New Lanark. The former manager saw it. I have not.

PW: Dorothy, enjoyed your story very much. Serendipity as well perhaps. https://ghosts.fandom.com/wiki/Malahide_Castle x

Catherine Maxwell Stuart

HAVING lived in a very very old house for the greater part of my life, I can honestly say I have never seen a ghost here despite desperately wanting to conjure one up when I was younger.

Now I feel more like I live comfortably with the spirits of Traquair and we don't have to intrude on one anothers lives. I have turned down endless requests from paranormal groups to come for overnight ghost hunts on the basis I don't want our peaceful spirits disturbed.

There was one night, however, when I was truly terrified at Traquair that I never divulge to visitors. Back in my teenage days I used to hang out with a gang of teenage boys and the odd cool girl as well. We rarely had the run of the house but one weekend, my parents were away and, of course, we planned a party. My friend Shona was going to spend the night and we decided we would sleep in the "haunted room."

There is a curious bedroom on the second floor called The Chintz Room. It was furnished with an old half tester bed, worn yellowing bed hangings and threadbare carpets. The room is wood panelled but unusually it also has a blocked corridor that runs all the way round it which does give rise to some interesting sound effects when the wind blows and whistles through the creaking wood.

It was used as a guest room. Various relatives would report having felt something there and a cousin reported waking up to see a lady leaning over him which my parents put down to his having a bad dream. Nevertheless, it was definitely a creepy room.

That night, after everyone had left, we headed upstairs a little drunkenly and got into the huge old creaking bed giggling and telling each other ghost stories and then finally tiring, we began to fall asleep. Suddenly, Shona pinched me and said,"Did you hear that?"

"What?" I replied.

"It was a footstep – I'm sure."

"You're just imagining it," I said, not remotely interested. "It's just the wind."

"No, definitely, I am sure it was a person," she insisted.

I tried to get back to sleep but a few minutes later I heard something odd that could have been a door closing. I was still unconvinced but we were both now wide awake.

Over the next hour or so we heard a few other strange noises but I couldn't decide if it was the wind or our imagination. A creaking door ("the wind"), a scratching sound ("must be mice"), a small thud ("the cat"). But the more I was trying to convince Shona that everything was normal, the more I started to think that there was something strange going on.

It seemed to be suddenly colder and I could tell Shona was getting increasingly worried so I tried to play it cool. But then I was quite sure when I heard footsteps too. For the first time we suddenly found ourselves holding hands under the covers.

Maybe it was a burglar – should we investigate? I decided against that course of action. Just a bit too risky.

Then the noises stopped and we began to relax. We joked a bit about scaring ourselves and finally tried going back to sleep.

Suddenly there was thumping almost above our heads and some minutes later we heard what definitely seemed like more than one set of foot steps. This time we were really frightened. In fact we were both sitting up in bed holding on to each other!

The footsteps suddenly got louder and more of them. They were coming from above, and now on the stairs, Now pounding along the corridor. I felt the colour drain from my face. It sounded as if a stampede was approaching and suddenly our door sprang open and into our room burst the entire group of friends we thought had left a couple of hours earlier.

Our faces must have registered extreme shock in that second before the reality dawned. It turned out our friends had never left and crept back upstairs to the top of the house where they spent nearly two hours planning their dastardly trick.

We had both been terrified and it cured my desire to even conjour up a ghost again. Yet I also knew that the spirits of Traquair would never act in such a mischievous way. It's just not in their nature.

DJ: Excellent Catherine! 😂

CS: Brilliant! I think that should go in the Traquair guide book C!

PW: Oh dear Catherine, some friends....

PW: I think your story fabulous and lucky you x

RM: Fun story Catherine. Sorry Lady Louisa isn't still around but then she knows Traquair is in good hands. x

BD: Fantastic story, Catherine! Bx

JM: Excellent tale & vividly told - historic

Traquair House Ale

Jonathan Gibbs

Fear Itself

THERE is a moment when watching the film Don't Look Now in the cinema, as the Hilary Manson character can be seen through a half-open door, sitting at a table.

This film concerns the supernatural, and many other aspects of life, love, loss & grief.

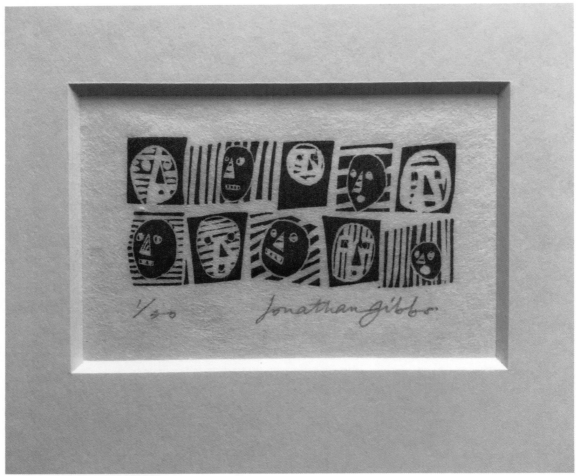

Wood engraving 30X70 mm.

At this moment, the clairvoyant sits and leans forward out of view beyond the door-frame. Watching the watchers, one can observe heads of the cinema audience moving together to the left, rather as tennis spectators move in unison, trying to see what is beyond the frame out of the camera-shot. Of course, this is a clever cinematography, as one is deceived by the artifice of the film director.

FEAR ITSELF is taken from the Franklin D. Roosevelt's inaugural address, as the title of the wood engraving. Much of the fear induced in films, and in literature results from what one cannot see, or hopes to see or dreads seeing, it is suggested, evoked to give a sense of suspense. We have nothing to fear, usually from the supernatural, and this wood engraving represents Halloween-like heads with exaggerated expressions of fear or astonishment

DJ: Comfort of Strangers! Another scary one - if I remember correctly.

JG: evoked to give a sense of suspense. We have nothing to fear, usually, from the supernatural, and my wood engraving represents Halloween-like heads, with exaggerated expressions of fear or astonishment. Incidentally, my apologies for such a late posting.

Andrew Brown

THIS is a true story. It begins with a trip to South America with my patron the art philanthropist Delfina Entrecanales. She had been invited to Buenos Aires in Argentina and Santiago in Chile by the ministers of culture of both those countries on an official visit because of her promotion of South American art in Europe.

As an adviser to her Foundation, she asked me if I'd like to come with her. Of course, I jumped at the chance as I had always wanted to go to Buenos Aries which turned out to be a marvellous town with, I might say, the most beautiful men in the world, I think, and very sexy. I got confused there for some Brazilian long haired footballer, so I had rather a great time.

Then we moved on to Santiago in Chile where we were looked after by the director of the Museum of Antiquities, an absolutely fascinating and charming man. It had been proposed that we should make a further trip through Patagonia, Southern Chile, down the Andes and eventually catch a boat in Punta Arenas, really a kind of lost town at the end of the world, and travel around Tierra del Fuego, "the land of fire."

Though I had enjoyed the early part, I wasn't entirely looking forward to this trip down the barren wasteland of Patagonia but one thing had enticed me. I had read many years ago Bruce Chatwyn's iconic travel book *In Patagonia*. He begins with the idea that when he was child, a distant cousin had discovered the remnants of a Mylodon, a giant prehistoric sloth in a cave in Patagonia. This had encouraged many other explorers to look for further prehistoric fossils there.

Because the cave's cold atmosphere up in the Andes was like a refrigerator, it had perfectly preserved the skin and scales and body of the Mylodon so much so that people thought it had only died very recently. But after a more recent examination, it was discovered it had probably died twenty or thirty thousand years ago and been preserved by the refrigerator- like cave.

This gave rise in the Edwardian period to a great interest in looking for supposedly extinct beasts. H. Rider Haggard's book *The Lost World* was based on this story of the Mylodon, bits of which are still in the Natural History Museum and eventually spawned Jurassic Park.

So as well as going to see penguin colonies and seal colonies, I was keen to go and visit the cave of the Mylodon, and I was further tempted because Delfina had said that we were going to fly from Santiago and stay in possibly the most expensive hotel in the world, the Torres del Paine National Park Hotel in the middle of a vast wilderness up several mountains with a view straight on to the Torres del Paine, which is the tail end of the Andes, the peaks of which had not been scaled until the 1970s. It was the flat plateau on top which had given H. Rider Haggard the idea of the lost world.

After a few days there, bird watching the giant condors and seeing the guanacos, a kind of llama, and never actually seeing any of the wild pumas, we were then going to Punta Arenas via a penguin colony. Delfina was not thrilled about this because she was, and is, diminutive, around about eighty years old, under five foot. When we arrived at a penguin colony, the giant penguins rushed up to her and stood round about as if she was a mother penguin, and just nestled into her Queen of the Penguins. I have photographs of this which for delicacies sake I will keep private.

She therefore felt less inclined to go to another penguin colony and I suggested that maybe we could go to the cave of the Mylodon and see the spot where the relics had been found. So she agreed to this and we arranged for a car to take us on the five hundred kilometre trip from the Torres del Paine Hotel to Punto Arenas, the port on the very south tip of Chile where we would get the cruise ship which would take us into the Antartic and round Cape Horn to Tierra del Fuego and finally dock in Ushuaia, the most southerly port in Argentina and get our flight back to Buenor Aires.

But when Delfina spoke to the driver in perfect Spanish, he told her that it was a tough drive to the Mylodon Cave and that if we drove there it would be difficult to get us to Punta Arenas for the evening and he thought we should really go as arranged to the penguin colony.

Delfina was fiercely resistant to visiting another penguin colony, but perhaps, because we had left so late after lunch in the afternoon, was there not a hotel half-way? she asked.

He thought about this - and we are talking about 300 kilometres of wilderness - more wild than Caithness and the moors of Northern Scotland. That's why so many Scots settled there and that is part of this story.

After some deliberation, he said, "Yes, there is an estancia half-way which takes paying guests. Would you like to go there? Shall I telephone them?"

He telephoned and it seemed they had a vacancy. So we drove for about two hours on the main road to Punta Arenas, then he suddenly went off onto a dirt track and for a half an hour through a stony, dusty wilderness and then suddenly in the distance we could see a patch of trees. Rising out of them was a strangely familiar looking building featuring wooden carved barge boards and a red tin roof. My initial thought was that it looked like a Scottish hunting lodge. I had time to do a drawing of it just before the light went surrounded by crumbling, rotten farm buildings, an abandoned windmill, and, for the first time in my life, I actually saw tumbleweed.

He drove up to a white picket fence and there was an overgrown garden with bushes and a paved path with grass and weeds growing through it. He picked up our suitcases, took them to the front door and put them down before retreating to the car, saying he would pick us up in the morning and take us to the Mylodon cave.

Delfina rang the front door bell and the door creaked open and there was what I can only describe, not unkindly, as a figure that looked like Lurch from the Addams family. He was about 6ft 7in tall, or more, dressed in black, with a bow tie and dishevelled black coat like a butler, and he said something gruntingly in Spanish to a rather disconcerted Delfina.

She replied and, suddenly, out of the shadowy vestibule came an elegant old lady dressed entirely in black wearing a chunky gold necklace who introduced herself in perfect English as the manageress of the estancia and told us that that we were welcome. When I asked her if there were any other guests, she said, "Oh no. Not many people get here. We are rather out of the way, you know"

Delfina asked if there was a restaurant nearby where we could go and have dinner. The manageress replied, "I'm sorry. Either two and a half hours back to Torres del Paine, or two and a half or three hours further to Punta Arenas, but she was very happy to provide dinner for us if that would be sufficient. We said, of course, having no choice.

Then she led us into a panelled wooden hall with a rather grand carved oak staircase, very Scottish in feeling, into a long wooden corridor which had several rooms off it. We were shown two. Delfina chose the slightly larger room and I chose the slightly smaller one with a single bed, both of which had enormous Victorian bathrooms off them with huge cast iron baths. There were enormous sinks and loads of Victorian furniture and accessories. Wash jugs and Victorian paintings hanging on the wall.

The lady asked if this was sufficient? We said more than sufficient, It was charming. Asked how all of this had come about, she said she would tell us at dinner and told us that dinner would be at 7pm.

By now, because we had left after 2pm to get there, it was about 5pm. The light was beginning to fade and I felt I wanted to get outside to do a drawing and have a walk around.

I asked if that would be alright, and she said, "Of course but it's in a sorry state now. This estancia used to be 300,000 acres full of sheep and workers. Now it's only 60,000 acres. What can you do with that? Only myself and Miguel, my butler, are still here."

Delfina and I dropped our things in our rooms and I took my drawing utensils and we walked out through the garden round into the back yards of the house where there were crumbling, decrepit wooden buildings, beautiful barns, shearing houses, a tilting windmill, and the proverbial tumbleweed. There was one lone dog howling in the wind.

After that we wandered back into the garden which was very overgrown, and in one corner there was a stone cairn, about 6ft high, with a flagpole on top of it. There was also a plaque, a stone tablet engraved to the memory of a Mr Mathieson and Mrs McColl, the same name as the famous sweet shop and newspaper shop in Edinburgh.

My memory, as this was about twelve years ago, is a bit hazy about some of the details but when I was recently looking for my drawings, a card fell out of my sketchbook and it gives the name of the place, the Hosteria Estancia Rio Penitente, Punta Arenas, and there inscribed upon the vard is the name Mariette, the gerente (the manageress).

We returned to our rooms and, as we were going up the unlit gloomy staircase, Delfina asked me what we should wear?

I said to her that I had brought my tartan trews and velvet jacket all the way from Britain and for the three weeks, almost a month, that we had been in South America, I had had no occasion to wear them.

She said, "Well, I've got a very nice evening dress and some jewellery that I haven't worn." She had also noticed that the lady was wearing some very nice jewellery.

We retired to our rooms and the lady told us that they did not have any electricity. Of course! However, they had a generator and Miguel, the butler, would put that on before it got dark. True to her word, the lights suddenly came on in our rooms as the dusk was falling and everything was brightly lit up in those beautiful Victorian bedrooms.

Both of us got ready. I knocked on Delfina's door just before 7pm and we both walked to the top of the wooden stairs and, as we started coming down them, we could see Mariette standing at the bottom.

We had gone no more than two or three steps when suddenly the lights went out and we were plunged into darkness. We moved another two steps and the lights went on. Another two steps and the lights went off. Moments later they came back on again, and Mariette said, "The ancestors are pleased to see you. They're not always pleased to see everyone, I can tell you!"

So Delfina and I continued down the stairs and at that point I noticed that some of the portraits which I had not see in the gloom of the hall before the lights went on, showed people dressed in kilts and Highland costumes and really, that the furnishings of the hall were perfect for a Victorian Scottish house. Mariette led us into a sitting room where there was more large Victorian heavy Scottish furniture, more portraits and photographs of people in Scottish garb and she explained to us that this house had been built by her husband's great grandfather and great grandmother who had come from Scotland in the 1890s, some of the first sheep farmers in the whole of Patagonia.

They had come here because it looked so much like the north of Scotland from which they came. They had become immensely wealthy and slowly from a log cabin, had built this large house, filled it full of Scottish antiques and had increased the estate to 300,000 acres.

Also, with the huge profits made from their sheep farming, they had managed to buy an estate in Scotland as well, and were able to travel in the autumn to Scotland for a month or so. And she said that arriving in tartan the way I had done was marvellous. It had raised her heart enormously, and also raised the hearts of the ancestors.

I asked what she meant by that and she said, "Well, you see, in the 1970s, under the Communist Allende Government, all the estates in Chile were nationalised and estates like this had dozens of families brought in to live on them. The Matheson family had left and gone to their house in Punto Arenas and had been very worried that all the paintings and eveything would be damaged.

I asked why it was therefore in such perfect condition? She said,"Bruce Chatwyn in his book talks about my mother-in-law and this estate. You see the gold necklace around my neck? This is the necklace he says her employees washed out of the river.

"What nonsense!" she continued. "These gold nuggets I am wearing around my neck, she bought from a jeweller's shop in Santiago. Chatwyn also says in the book that when they had to abandon the estate, she took all the valuables with her and packed them away.

"Not true! Everything was left. There was no time to pack and take anything away. A posse of men arrived, ejected her from the house and brought the families in."

"So how come everything is OK? "I asked. "They didn't damage anything? I think that is extraordinary."

"That is because the ancestors would not let them," she explained. "No family ever was able to sleep in this house for more than one night. It's absolutely true.

"The first group of families who were billeted here left the next morning saying that the place was haunted. A few days later, another group of families arrived. After one night, they too refused to stay. After several attempts at it, the Commissar for the region decided that the house was truly haunted and everyone was afraid to come anywhere near it.

"So this was the only estancia in the whole of Chile that was left untouched because no one would come near it or touch anything in it. When the Allende Government was over, we were given the house back."

And at that point, she admitted she was not the Manageress but a member of the family. "My mother-in-law was the lady in the Chatwyn book," she told us. "That book is so inaccurate," she added.

I said to her that I wanted to go to the Cave of the Mylodon, and she said, "Please do not bother. There is nothing to see. It is just a pile of rubble. It is a difficult drive and a long walk and I think Madam Entrecanales might not be interested," adding "but there's a very lovely penguin colony nearby. Maybe you should go and see that?"

Delfina refused to go to another penguin colony

Anyway, we had dinner with Mariette in a dining room that was entirely Scottish with blue and white willow pattern plates, silver, Edinburgh crystal. Everything was delightful. Excellent food. As in all of South America, it was steak and chips, no fruit and next to no vegetables.

After dinner and a glass of whisky, we retired to bed and Mariette gave us both a torch and said, "Now will it be alright if I give you half an hour to make your ablutions? Then we will turn the generator off."

So we went straight up, very tired as you can imagine, and got into our bedrooms, said goodnight to each other, washed, brushed teeth, undressed, got into bed, a book at my side for a bit. In fact, the book was In Patagonia and I was reading the bit about Mariette's mother-in-law when the lights went off. I picked up the torch beside my bed to see if it worked, and lay down in the darkness, very tired and ready to fall asleep when, suddenly, there were footsteps, the sounds of somebody walking heavily around my room. I grabbed the torch and turned it on.

Nothing. There was nobody there. I thought that maybe I was half-dreaming and turned over to go to sleep again.

Once more there were crashing footsteps. Torch back on, and again there was nobody there.

I went into the bathroom and checked. The bathroom windows were barred. My bedroom windows were fastened sash windows with a catch. My door was locked with a key. which I had turned behind me. I listened to hear if I could hear anything from Delfina. Nothing again.

Back into bed. I put off the light. Crash"! Crash! Crash! I concluded perhaps there must be another floor above and it must be Miguel, the butler, getting ready for bed and it was his footsteps I was hearing.

With that, as I thought, I fell asleep. I'm not quite sure if that was the case but then the ancestors came.

They came one by one, sat on my bed and told me their stories of botched abortions, incarcerations in mad houses, petty hatreds between members of the family, exclusions from Wills, abuse of children. They told me everything, all night.

In the morning, I was exhausted. When Delfina knocked on my door and I got up to open it, I asked her if she had heard anything in the night?

"No, "she said. "Not a thing,"

No footsteps. Nothing. "I fell asleep immediately,"she said."Let's go downstairs for breakfast."

I quickly dressed and walked downstairs into the dining room for a marvellous breakfast - sausage, bacon and eggs, black pudding, everything had been prepared on the sideboard.

Mariette was there and she said, "How did you sleep?"

"Well, I think I met your ancestors," I said. "Did one have a teddy bear? Did one have a pet dog? Did one wear a white rose?"

Whereupon she brought out a photograph of a group of people most of whom I had seen that night. "I thought they'd like you," she said. "They don't mean any harm. All they want to do is talk.

"They often talk to me but those stupid Communists who took over the house weren't willing to talk to them."

The car that came for us that morning was scheduled to take us to the Mylodon Cave but I was exhausted, and Delfina had lost interest.

Instead, we decided to go straight to Punta Arenas where we were to meet Mariette's son Jaimie, who looked exactly like Gomez from The Addams Family, with slick black hair, a dinner suit and little moustache.

When I had asked Mariette what he did for a living, she told me he owned all the cemeteries in Chile. "And the cemetery in Punto Arenas is the second most famous in the world after Recoleta in Buenos Aires. It's immensely grand," she said proudly.

And I can tell you that it is. It is listed among the ten best cemeteries in the world.

As we had said goodbye to Mariette at the door of the Estancia Rio Penitente, she had announced, "It's not goodbye. You will be back and even if I am dead, I will still be here to meet you!"

So that was how Delfina and I ended our trip to Punto Arenas, staying overnight and catching the boat around Cape Horn to Tierra del Fuego in the morning. But that is another story.

PW: How did you come by that brilliant group photograph Andrew? Beautifully researched storyxx

AB: In researching this story I looked on-line and found a recent advertisement for the Hosteria Estancia Rio Penitente including this family photo and showing the house and farm buildings restored and it has now been turned into a proper hotel. When I asked Mariette why she was taking paying guests, she had said, "Because we were impounded in the Communist era, my mother-in-law and I were always worried it would happen again."

"But commercial businesses were not impounded so the people who owned hotels did not have their properties taken. It was only the estates and mansion houses, so we felt that we should start taking paying guests and call ourselves a hotel, and that way escape the estancia being stolen in the future."

Join

Pat Watson

FOR me there has always been a sense of another layer of existence of time, not tangible, more like ethereal and transient like the clouds. My mother also had this sense of life but most certainly not my father who heartily disapproved of 'any such nonsense'.

My story for you today is 'Pie Ann'.

Alan and I bought a very lovely cottage in Ladybank in 1987. It required some remedial work. For a time we rented a lodge at Kincaple, near St Andrews. That was a very lovely time in our life. Alan would take the last train home from Ladybank to Leuchars and walk to Kincaple after an evening working on our cottage called Lochgorm (Blue Loch).

Andrew came by one time to visit us in Ladybank and I remember driving him either to Markinch or Kirkcaldy for his train. The car's brakes developed a fault. I had to work with the clutch and handbrake to slow the car. That was excruciating, no wonder he didn't visit again until last year with Michael doing the driving! My brother came to my rescue but I had to drive his spitfire. My goodness that was an experience… Those were the days.

Lochgorm was a lovely stone built cottage with a very large inaccessible back garden. At some point there had been an informal arrangement for access which new owners of the neighbouring house refused to honour. Goodness knows why because it wouldn't have inconvenienced them at all.

This cottage had the most efficient underfloor ventilation, and we would see our occasional table floating when the strong winds arrived like we have been having this last wee while. Alan's father suggested we brick up the vents when the strong winds arrived that blow the sand all over the beautiful Howe of Fife. The vent in the kitchen extension allowed sand from the field through the vents and the kitchen would be coated in a fine dusting of sand. The roof was nail sick so that added to our difficulties. But we liked it very much. However when our third child arrived, we decided we needed to move home for more space.

When Moira was born, sometimes of an evening, Alan in his studio, I would hear the cry of a child. I always went to check on the little ones who would be quite settled.

One evening, Alan's birthday I think, a friend offered to babysit for us, a very rare evening out. We went to the local pub but didn't enjoy it. We decided to pop by the bowling club rather than return home too early. It was much nicer than the local hostelry and friendlier. We sat with people from our street and we got to chatting about the history of our house and Ladybank. This neighbour told us our house was where Pie Ann, a baker, had lived with her husband. They had a baby daughter who died. I think possibly leukaemia. Alan's not here to help me with the memory of things.

They were heart broken. Often when I would go for coal, I would feel the presence of a very sad man in the shed. There was a tooling work surface in this shed. It was good to have an explanation and somehow the upset child and father were no longer troubling to us.

Supernatural from an old *Chambers Dictionary*: 'Above or beyond nature; not according to the course of nature; miraculous; spiritual.'

For me, it is the unexplained energy of life over which I have no control.

PW: Thank you Dorothy. I have missed everything from Friday to Anne's note from Dalai Lama. Anne is my first-born daughter and works for sound festival Aberdeenshire. I think it is so sad if we lose the best of ourselves which is the arts over the back of this terrible time.

RM: Absolutely Pat. Not unlike the story of Rev. Charlie Robertson of Canongate Kirk and the baby under the door stone. X

BD: Excellent, Pat. Very interesting story! Barbara.

PW: all.

PW: They are okay xx

CMS: Enjoyed your story Pat – we are never alone.

PW: Thank you Catherine, I don't ever go looking though. Hope all is well with you all.

ACT OF FAITH

Callum Stark

IN the vein of a 'test of faith', I am divulging something to Decameron that very few know about me and most are shocked to discover: I was a born-again Christian.

First, however, came my decision – aged eight and inspired by my glorious great aunt – to become a Buddhist. With all the zeal of the convert, I persuaded my parents to buy me a fairly substantial Buddha statue and, according to my primary teacher, burst into the school library one morning demanding to see every book on the subject the librarian could muster.

What's more, I even took on the mantle of pint-sized evangelist, convincing two of my little friends that Buddhism was for them also, the only path to enlightenment.

In retrospect, however, I see that much like my great aunt, my 'faith' comprised nothing more than a collection of hollow ideals. And, as my Mum would remind me, temper tantrums were hardly compatible with enlightenment.

Time passed; I lost interest, only to become – aged 11 – passionately interested in Christianity. An odd choice given my upbringing by two staunchly atheist parents and a wider family with a very complicated relationship to organised religion. And yet, I can still remember what it was that lit my ecclesiastical touch paper: the novel *I Capture the Castle* by Dodie Smith!

It's been years since I've read it but I seem to recall some sort of romantic assignation in a village church; this was enough to set my mind ablaze with images of high holy glamour and off I toddled the following morning to church, accompanied by my grandmother's elegant friends with their pearls and pink rinses.

Perhaps unsurprisingly, my faith was flimsy and eventually fleeting: I was always more interested in the spectacle and ceremony rather than what the minister was actually saying (for that reason it puzzles me why I plumped for the low Church of Scotland over the high of Catholicism – kids are often irrational, I suppose). And yet, in spite of or perhaps because of this, I continued to go – comforted by the practice if not the faith. And still I go, once or twice a year – I find it like a form of meditation.

Speaking of meditation, I am once again gripped by the principles of Buddhism, though perhaps slightly more earnestly ten years on. I attend classes at a temple in Leith run by Samye Lyng and taught by a highly tempestuous shaven-headed nun, who often gets into embittered arguments with her students.

After my first class, I inadvertently discovered that my teacher – in the '60s – was a top fashion model and the long-term girlfriend of footballer George Best; she was inspired to renounce her previously hedonistic life of partying with the Beatles and Roman Polanski after hearing the Dalai Lama speak at the Royal Albert Hall.

Such a tale (or parable, rather) perhaps illustrates the power of faith, the likes of which I don't, or don't yet, have.

RM: I spent the early part of my life in South East Asia and my mother always insisted that Buddhism was the only religion that respected women. Even so, I was brought up a hardened Presbyterian, tracing my ancestry directly back to John Knox's Sinclair aunt at Morham - Knox a much maligned and deliberately (by the Kirk) misinterpreted man who, contrary to his misogynist reputation, rather liked women (having two wives and two daughters upon whom he doted). Despite the reportage, as malignant then as it is now, he even had a healthy regard for Mary Queen of Scots and her Hepburn husband, having grown up with him as his tenant.

As for I Capture the Castle, it is also my very favourite book as Andrew will confirm, with Dodie Smith modelling it on Glen. Brilliant. What more can I say?

CS: Fount of knowledge Roddy! I know little of John Knox more than, as you say, the view of him as rather unpleasant misogynist and from going round his house in the High Street. I was given I Capture the Castle to read by my granny, as it was her favourite book as a child, and I loved it. Must re-read it. And I never knew she based it on Glen. We can discuss this in detail.

PW: Hi Callum, a very thoughtful contribution. Thank you.

BD: Interesting piece Callum. Children often have serious thoughts on the subject of 'why are we here?'

RM: Adults too Barbara xxx

CMS: Another rare insight! And I Capture the Castle also a big favourite of mine. I saw the Dalai Llama at Samye Ling some years ago and he was very much of the view we should choose whichever religion suits us best.

Andrew Brown

AFTER my failed attempt to enter the priesthood as a teenager, and because the Bishop of Galloway exerted me to go forth and serve the Lord through art, I have since put my faith in the power and restoration and value of art.

This belief has never been shaken or needed testing though on one memorable occasion my knowledge of art was put to the test very publicly on television.

It was in the early '90s and I had been invited by George Melly to take part in a quiz program called "Gallery" which he hosted with the artist Maggie Hambling. You were shown a tiny square of a famous painting and had to guess what it was, earning fewer points the more the painting was disclosed and incurring penalty points for guessing wrongly.

The hosts took it very seriously and excoriated players who took a punt early on and were incorrect. On my first appearance on the program the first picture was represented by a square inch of canvas showing a single pebble and without hesitation, I said I know what the painting is. Maggie was scornful and pointed out that if I was wrong as I undoubtedly would be, I would get maximum penalty points and be out of the competition before it started.

So it was an enormous leap of faith in my artist intuition to stick to my guns and declare the almost totally obscured painting was *Pegwell Bay* by William Dyce. To the chagrin of the doubters, the whole picture slowly came into view and I was proved right, receiving maximum points for the first time in the program's history.

I'm still not certain how I did it, perhaps because Dyce painted in tempera the pebble had a translucent sheen and because Hayley's Comet was depicted in the painting, it had made a deep impression on me.

My unexpected success got me invited back several more times and though I acquitted myself well, I never repeated my early achievement and eventually George Melly complained that my flashy suits were overshadowing his and I was dropped from the program.

Marie-Louise Brulatour Mills

THE sheer white curtain blows and covers its marble presence on the side table. For a moment it appears to be an anonymous carved alabaster form shrouded by a veil.

I gently lift the curtain and a statue of St. Joseph is revealed. I sit down and sink into the worn cushion of the armchair to reflect.

"If you want to sell a house you must get a statue of St. Joseph and put him nose down in the earth facing the front door," my cousin wrote in an email. My initial thought was she was going mad? How could such a superstition create a sale?

Having been at convent schools all my life and never hearing about this particular aspect of "How Catholics sell their homes," I was indeed flabbergasted.

My initial reaction after is, "What?", followed by a thoughtful,"Why not?" the latter being my normal mantra.

Where does one find a statue of St. Joseph in the South of France? While there are many churches, there is no shop that sells religious icons. At least I didn't know of any.

I asked one of my house agents, a young Swedish girl, and her Russian partner who promised to bring me to a small church nearby called Notre Dame de Laghet to see, experience it and to buy a small statue.

They picked me up and we tootled around the mountains to finally arrive at the Sanctuary. The three levelled church was flooded with thanksgiving memorabilia, the usual silver medallions and paintings that depicted the miracles had a charm but felt nothing until we went down to the crypt. I had just begun my ascent, not even reaching the gates of the sacristy, and I felt a strange sensation. Tears began to well up and while I didn't understand, I knew this sudden heat and vibrations of my body meant that a sanctified presence and energy was here.

After some prayers and supplications to sell my home, which had become a financial necessity as well as an emotional one to make my last move, we turned and went back upstairs to the ground floor and crossed a space that led to the shop.

I asked the nun for a statue of St. Joseph. She brought out a large ugly one for 120 euros, which shocked me. The market value was less than ten, I am sure. I decided to poke around the store wading through the endless statues, medals, rosary beads and paintings of more saints. While these crowded corners were less than enticing, I wandered around long enough to find a small alabaster statue of St. Joseph holding a baby Jesus. It crossed my mind that decades ago it might have been of St. Christopher before he was demoted as a saint but it did say something to me, and for twelve euros it was mine.

I can only asume that the nun, who was ready to sell me anything, was both disappointed as well as relieved after poking around for twenty minutes.

I did as my cousin told me and buried the statue nose down in a pot full of earth facing my front door. While hard to comprehend within an hour four agents called for me to bring potential buyers to view my home with its extraordinary panoramic views in the turn-of-the-century building.

Curious, I thought.

A few weeks later without a sale, I spoke to my banker, an Italian from Rome. I explained this strange ritual. which she knew all about and suggested I get another statue to put in another spot. Soon after another package arrived and I decided to change the sunken positions, as the actual front door and the front of my place were different. The two statues exchanged positions, like pushing a refresh button on the computer.

Within one single hour my neighbour called and asked if she could come with her beau of the moment to show him my place in the historic building. She took him around and I made coffee and, before his first sip, he asked the price. I told him, adding that I would not haggle. That was it!

"I'll take it," he said, finished his coffee, and left.

RM: Great story Marie Louise. You. Must show me St Joseph when I next visit.ditto Dorothy. Equally getting bored but I still have faith this too shall pass - soon please.

DJ: Hope so Roddy!

PW: I enjoyed your story very much Marie-Louise, must bear this in mind when I come to sell this house, xx

ML: Thanks so much but it's all true 🧎🧎🗿🗿🗿😊🙏🎶😳😳😳

Dorothy Jackson

I envy people who have a strong faith. During this pandemic, we have been asked to put our faith in science. We have also been encouraged to have faith in the judgements made by our politicians.

At the start of this stressful period, I went with all of this. I was stoic and believed that we were all working together to get over this horrible virus. As the weeks have gone on I have started to lose my faith in both the scientists and politicians. It saddens me that I think that way as I would always have said that I would follow the science.

But I feel, increasingly, that they are perhaps not being allowed to make their own decisions. I hate all that political point scoring and appreciate that our First Minister is speaking from her heart and her genuine concern for her people.

I remember clearly the outbreak of Ecoli 0157 in Wishaw in 1996. It is still the world's largest recorded outbreak. Twenty-one people died and many were left with permanent conditions. I knew some of these people. Many were elderly as the main outbreak was in a Pensioners' Lunch at a church.

Another outbreak was in a Care Home. So like Covid 19, the elderly were worse affected. Not all were older but the younger did recover better. And not all were affected. Even at that time, a track and trace was put into play, hampered because not all the facts were available.

Time was of the essence and I'm sure the faith of the minister and parishioners was severely challenged at this time. They were burying friends and wondering when it would end. The stress relating to this outbreak continued and was re-lived when the Fatal Accident Enquiry report was published a couple of years later.

I am weary of this pandemic and a bit negative for the future. I need to get out of this phase. I love books and knitting and have passed my time happily in the garden since we have had such lovely weather. I'm so glad for Billy's company and feel for those who are on their own and waiting for the next lifting of the restrictions. I'm desperate to see my son Andrew and hopefully this will be soon. I'm fed up with the backbiting and arguing.

As I said at the start, we have had to have faith in the politicians and scientists but not blind faith. We are constantly facing a barrage of information which we read and then, briefly think we can get a handle on this. I read somewhere that a mum was trying to explain to her child why there was a need to wash their hands thoroughly. She explained that the virus was like glitter – and when you think of this you realise how hard it is to get rid of glitter. It gets everywhere!

DJ: I hope my contribution isn't too negative! It's how I'm feeling at the moment.

PW: Oh Dorothy, with you on all of this. My daughter, partner and son have been cooped up in a city centre flat. She is home with her son as I have a garden. I can see the toll it has taken. Let's hope something happens soon to help with all of this, thank you for sharing your thoughts xx

CMS: Have to have faith, Dorothy, that we will finally come out the other side eventually!

DJ: Thanks Catherine. I think I wrote this on a dull day! I'm usually quite upbeat.

Jonathan Gibbs

XEROX MAN wood engraving 75 X 100mm. A Test of Faith ---

THIS appears to be a narrative illustration, perhaps destined for the pages of a book. But this is not the case. It was commissioned to demonstrate the fidelity of the Rank Xerox photocopy.

At school and art college, we used to have illustrated talks about the History of Art. This meant slides of the works of Piero Della Francesca, Gwen John, Mark Rothco for example, or indeed William Dyce. Much of my art historical knowledge has been gained from these projected reproductions.

When I saw actual paintings on museum or gallery walls, I was astonished, a revelation.

Hockney has written about the revelation upon seeing the first high-quality reproductions of paintings in Skira art books, by which he means that these give a much more accurate and authentic picture of the picture in question.

I have always believed that the word 'illustration' is misunderstood, and often used to mean very different things. All the illustrations I have ever made in the truest sense have been intended for reproduction. The original artwork, always a wood engraving, is not important, once an accurate scan has transferred it into its printed/reproduced form, as faithfully as possible.

I was amazed to see an original drawing by Aubrey Beardsley in the V&A, having known his work from the Yellow Book, and all those posters. These reproductions are clear and sharp, black and white, with fine line and flat blacks..

However, Beardsley's pen and ink drawing seen in actuality was covered with imperfections and changes of mind, by the artist, mistakes, all of which had been painted out with 'process-white.' Or inked over with Indian ink, and I could see the scratch marks of Beardsley's nib, and the smudges.

Publishers and printers had made sure that the printed version was sharp and without blemishes. Beardsley knew that his work was for the printed page.

Likewise, Quentin Blake's original drawings for the BFG have pieces of paper pasted over the mistakes, with a new drawing on top. Blake's art editor can deal with these imperfections with Photoshop. The whole point of painting and drawing is the actual object, from my point of view anyway. Which is to say, to understand the piece you must see it in the flesh, in actuality.

Nowadays students will say, 'I know so-and-so's work very well..' I know I have spoken such words too. But they have often only seen the work in reproduction, or on a screen, a website, Instagram, WhatsApp, or suchlike. A pale imitation, with no fidelity whatsoever to the original piece of work.

But Hockney also mentions that it is better to have a reproduction, however poor, of the artist's work, rather than none. His example for this point of view is The Baptism of Christ by Piero, which is in the National Gallery. Hockney has a postcard of this masterpiece, A6, pinned up in his studio. A miniature reproduction, an illustration.

But he also spoke of the marvellous and profound qualities of the original.

Back to the Xerox Man at the start of this piece. I was asked to use extremely fine line-work by the commissioning designer to show that a photocopy by Xerox could reproduce it perfectly. The photocopy was placed beside my original print to show the fidelity of production. Up to a point.

However, it was just a copy.

Mark Muller Stuart – Act of Faith

Keeping Faith with the Rule of Law and Peace-making

WHEN I think of acts and tests of faith, I think of law and how our compliance with it implicitly rests on our faith that others – particularly those tasked with its enforcement – will respect it. You find out a lot about a person and a state's commitment to the rule of law in times of conflict.

The Rule of Law

AS I noted earlier, in the early 1990s I was involved in bringing a series of cases before the European Commission of Human Rights about Kurdish village destruction in south-east Turkey. I remember trying to convince Kurdish villagers to bring actions against the Turkish Government. They looked at me as if I was mad. "There's a war going on here, Mr Muller, don't you see it?" their representatives would scream at me.

But over time they succumbed out of desperation. In the event we brought hundreds of cases that led to the Turkish Government paying out millions of Lire but not without our first claimant being assassinated.

These cases would shine a spotlight on the attrocities that the Turkish Government did not want Europe to see. But what I remember most is one of the earlier cases concerning the destruction of the small town of Lice when everything hung in the balance.

It was 1995 and we were at a fact-finding hearing of the European Commission of Human Rights in Ankara into events at Lice. The applicant was an eighty-year old peasant and father of eight children who had petitioned against the execution of one of his sons who had simply been tending to his vineyard when the soldiers passed by in their vehicles.

On seeing the soldiers, the son downed his tools and ran across the field into the forest for cover. The soldiers stopped and gave chase. The old man watched in mounting horror as the soldiers fanned out in an attempt to catch their prey.

A few minutes later he heard gunfire coming from the little forest by the vineyard.The Applicant hid until the soldiers had gone. When he got to the forest, he found his son dead amongst the leaves. Around him lay strewn government issued bullets and Turkish cigarette butts.

Later on, the Applicant was forced to join the other residents of Lice in the town square. He tried to complain about the murder of his son. However, the governor claimed he'd been killed by the PKK. For three years, we waited in Ankara for the old man to appear before the Commission to give his evidence.

We had just spent four days examining Turkish generals about the incident to their utter astonishment at having to appear in their own Capital in a Chamber of their own State Security Building to account for actions against a people they claimed didn't even exist. They denied the incident of course but we didn't have a case without the father.

But where was he? Had he lost faith? Had he been killed?

He lived a thousand miles to the east. We had made frantic efforts to locate him and were on the verge of calling it a day when an extraordinary moment occurred. The two large doors suddenly opened. A wizened old man walked into the enormous Chamber. This bedraggled wrinkled figure took his crumpled cap off his head in a gesture of immediate respect to the Commission and slowly made his way in dead silence to the middle of the room where a single witness chair was placed.

He was flanked each side by lawyers and state officials of the Republic of Turkey. He began by apologising for his late arrival. He told the Commission how he had been threatened with death if he gave evidence and how the soles of his daughters' feet had been beaten as a warning against his intended act of testimony.

He confirmed how he had been forcibly stopped at Diyarbakir Airport from taking a flight to Ankara but had managed to hide himself on a bus.

It soon became clear to all and sundry that there was little that the State could now do to this eighty-year old man, caught in the twilight of his life but demonstratively convulsed by the horror of his beloved son's death. It had taken him over 70 hours to reach Ankara.

Then began the spiteful cross-examination of the Turkish state lawyers. "How many soldiers came to the town?" one brayed.

"A lot," replied the old man.

"Don't play with this Court," said another. "Numbers count. This is a Court of Law."

The old man couldn't read or count. "A lot. I don't know – a million," the old man finally replied.

"Ahah!" omitted the lawyer turning around in triumph to the Judges.

But then the Commission President Nicholas Bratza QC began asking a series of quiet uncomplicated questions. His elegant inquiry burnt itself onto my memory.

"What clothes did they wear? What cigarettes did they smoke? What colour were the vehicles? What did the bullets look like? What sort of boots did they wear? What accents did they have?" And so on.

I have never witnessed such a quietly understated but utterly devastating inquiry into the truth. It was a testament to the power of the European Convention and the rule of law. It constituted a small but telling act of civilisation which silenced all the advocates in the Chamber.

Bratza had elicited the unvarnished truth about an unvarnished small town from an unvarnished man who remained utterly untouched by the larger politics and implications of his unadorned testimony.

The attack on Lice was to have huge consequences in Europe. During 1993, enraged Kurds who had sought refuge from Turkey took to the streets across Europe in protest at the attack on Lice. The protests led to a string of violent attacks on Turkish installations in Germany that in turn led to the PKK being designated as a terrorist organisation by the German Government.

These protests had been directed towards Germany and other NATO countries as their weapons had been deployed against defenceless villagers. The attack on October 22, 1993, on the people of Lice constituted the Kurd's Guernica, and left an indellible mark on all concerned.

But I, for one, will never forget Nicholas Bratza's devastating lesson to that Turkish state lawyer about what the rule of law is all about. For it lies not in clever words or in the form of a case but also in the treatment of substance.

But form is also important when it comes to the faith in the rule of law. This was exemplified by another case I acted in before the European Court in 2013 on behalf of an ETA female prisoner convicted of multiple murders, who had her prison term extended after a parole rule limiting prison sentences to thirty years was redefined unlawfully by the Spanish Supreme Court in an attempt to stop ETA members convicted in the 1990s from ever being released.

I was asked to represent her after a secret peace deal that brought the ETA conflict to an end, which included a clause concerning prisoners, was ditched by the new right-wing Spanish Government that had recently been elected.

It was an electrifying case with emotions running high on both sides. If we won, 75 of the most high-profile ETA convicts would be released.

We had received intelligence that the equivalent of the Spanish Home Secretary had secretly met with the President of the Court in an attempt to lobby him. I had to decide whether to raise this and blow a hole in the credibility of the Court or keep faith in its commitment to the rule of law.

I kept silent and we won the case. All eyes now turned on the Spanish judiciary after the Government said it should not enforce the judgement. It was a huge day for the rule of law across Europe. Over 200,000 people crammed onto the streets of Madrid to protest against the European Court judgement, while a further 80,000 celebrated on the streets of San Sebastian.

In the event, the judiciary ordered the release of seventy-five ETA prisoners despite huge pressure from the Spanish government. The next day, the right-wing press ran a story about the terrorists' lawyer and his castle.

Little did they know that all the case conferences had been convened in the first library at Traquair where the 7th Earl of Traquair had earlier lamented his disastrous trips to Madrid where his beloved wife died in 1796 after he tried unsuccessfully to court the Spanish king into giving him a series of mining concessions.

Faith in Peace-Making
THE case taught me not to put too much faith in politicans. I had learnt earlier not to do that after putting faith in David Cameron after he confidentially told a colleague of mine that he 'would do all he could' to support his attempts to win justice and compensation for bombing victims of IRA Semtex supplied by Gaddafi.

His words encouraged us to go to Benghazi in March 2011 during the height of the Libyan conflict to negotiate a compensation agreement with the new rebel leader who had promised to receive us. We got the agreement which was hailed by the UK Envoy on the ground only for the PM to go back on his word when he refused to act on it. It later emerged that MI6 had been working with moderate loyalists of Gaddafi all along, and this was just a distraction. It is interesting how a rebel leader kept his word but our own one did not.

Peace deals like law cannot be made without us also testing our faith in the word of others.

I will also remember in 2014 putting my faith in a Russian sympathising citizen journalist who arranged for me to meet the leaders of the Russian backed Donetsk People's Republic in Eastern Ukraine in order to solicit a pause in fighting and to try to release hostages on behalf of a humanitarian organisation.

I was taken to a lonely riverbank where I was bundled into the back of a dark van. At that moment, we had no idea whether they would kill us or not.

We emerged into the barbed-wired compound of the Donetsk administrative building that the rebels had taken over and where we knew on the 11th floor there was a torture chamber. Their leader's office was on the 12th floor.

The walk up the stairs was one of the longest of my life. I can't tell you how relieved I was when they took us past the offices on the 11th floor with its picture of Obama with a moustache and the plaited hair of Julia Timoshenko.

As faith would have it, we got the pause in the fighting from the rebel Russian intelligence leader who, somewhat ironically, was later killed by his own in mysterious circumstances, perhaps one floor down from where we all stood.

Unlike Cameron, he at least kept his word and, in so doing, renewed my faith in the capacity of people to put trust in others even in the most unlikely of circumstances.

Without such trust and the testing and keeping of faith, there can be no peace, let alone law.

In Bengazi in April 2011 with UK Special Envoy
after negotiating an agreement with Libyan rebels.

Catherine Maxwell Stuart

MY Roman Catholic upbringing came with a lot of baggage; the heritage of a family that upheld their faith for centuries against all the odds; parents that were dedicated practising Catholics and with a fervent desire to ensure that I was properly religiously educated. All this wrapped in a blanket of Catholic guilt that I hadn't been sent off to a good Convent boarding school.

I reviled everything about Catholicism when I was a child. From being forced into a dress and marched off every Sunday to the old priest who used to spend just too long staring at me from the altar. As a teenager, I was sent off to a Catholic Youth Group where young student priests from the nearby seminary, Drygrange, used to pitch up with guitars and flared trousers to some worthy local parishioner's house. I would then embark on some long argument about a woman's right to abortion, and the evenings would finally culminate with "open" confession held in the host's bedroom!

The final straw was the new priest who arrived at our Church (c.1975). In he swept with his slicked back hair and a guitar in hand. He delivered a Mass like it was a Shakespearean soliloquy. Women flocked, the congregation doubled, a folk club was formed but I couldn't help thinking it was all phoney.

Somehow I was persuaded to go with a group to a charismatic renewal meeting in the Usher Hall in Edinburgh, which was all the rage at the time. This was Catholicism with even more theatre and a touch of the supernatural; literally hundreds of devotees began speaking "in tongues" including our priest, for hours on end.

That signalled the end of any faith I had in the Catholic Church or desire to find any faith for another decade.

It was not until I came across some more radical Catholics at the Edinburgh Chaplaincy that my interest was re-ignited by the doctrine of liberation theology in Latin America. As I was planning to go to Central America, I found myself agreeing to visit a co-operative that the Chaplaincy funded in El Salvador

I had not realised that this was in the guerilla controlled north of the country so my trip involved being smuggled in the boot of a car through various military checkpoints. However, what I experienced there were priests acting as revolutionaries, health workers and genuinely doing good work. This, I thought, was what Catholicism should be all about.

Then about twenty years later I met a remarkable priest called Roland Walls who led a religious community at Roslin where he had commandeered a corrugated shed that had been an ex-miners' library with his "brothers", who lived in wooden huts in a small ramshackle garden. He had been an Anglican priest but converted to Catholicism later in life which led him to being ostracised by his former colleagues.

He had a deep intellect and ability to communicate the most complex theological ideas with a simplicity and clarity that was awe inspiring. His faith was utterly authentic and he had a great sense of humour.

He made me think of some of the extraordinary priests who lived at Traquair over the centuries and their devoted followers. The Chaplain who was here during the attack by the Protestant mob from Peebles in 1688 but continued to serve the family. The priest who was here in 1812 when the congregation was pelted with stones as they left the house – Mass was still being held at the time in a little chapel at the top of the house.

And there was Fr William Wallace who was here when the Catholic Emancipation Act was finally passed.

An old lady in Peebles told my father about her grandparents who had walked the hills from Selkirk (around 16 miles) barefoot, carrying their shoes in order to be married by Fr Wallace at the Traquair Chapel.

Last September, a group of us rode over to Hawick to commemorate the 175th anniversary of the first Catholic church being founded in Hawick (by Fr Wallace) and coming over the hills with some born-in-the-saddle horsemen of Hawick that were part of the small Catholic parish there, I found myself enjoying being part of this old religion so bound up with our past and reflecting that even if I still lack faith, there is something inspiring about those who do.

Roddy Martine

MY name is Pongo. I am an Orangutan For those who have never before seen or heard of me, perhaps I should explain. I am a large ginger monkey from the island of Borneo in the South China Seas.

I am very special. My wife says I look like Prince Harry.

I was born into a land and a religion where nothing ever dies; everything mortal is immortal. With parallels to Buddhism, the Animism belief we follow tells us that everything in our evolving circle of life – birth, death and re-birth – is part of the universe, part of the whole, part of our destiny.

But for the last half of a century that destiny has been on hold.

For generations, we Orangutans pursued our modest, uncomplicated existence deep within the Borneo rain forest, left to our own devices among the high tops of densely impenetrable vegetation which once upon a time umberellad our ancestral habitat. For as long as any of us can remember our neighbours, the Dyak tribes, the Chinese and Malay humans, the Rajahs and the Tuans, honoured us. They left us alone knowing we meant no harm. Nor did the other animals of the forest bother us. They know we are vegetarians.

Then half a century ago came the Malaysian and Indonesian takeover. These colonials were hungry for wealth to finance their cities and their lifestyles. They plundered our vast acreages of timber; our homeland was transformed into endless palm oil plantations. The poachers came and stole our children to sell as pets to Europeans and Americans. Over the past forty years, 60 per cent of our natural habitat has been destroyed.

The burning, the logging, the deforestation continues. Alas, it has only been recently that somebody has said stop! And that is where our faith comes into play.

So many of my loved ones have gone – uncles, aunts, brothers and sisters, cousins and kinfolk. The truth is they had nowhere else to go. Since 1999, an estimated one hundred and fifty of us have disappeared. It made us begin to think everyone had forgotten about us.

But we always knew in our hearts that an intelligent, caring world would ultimately rally to our cause. After all, we share 97per cent of the same DNA.

Where there is faith there is hope. From the Western World in 1971 came Save the Orangutan in partnership with the Borneo Orangutan Foundation (BOSF). Then came the fantasy author Sir Terry Pratchett with a television documentary – although I was far from impressed when he said I had a face like "a surprised coconut."

Engaging the bees, also an endangered species, the World Wildlife Fund has just launched a sustainable honey business on the island to support us.

So there is hope even though I sometimes feel, in fact I know, that this is just the beginning of our fight for survival. We must have faith.

Ten years ago the British actress Joanna Lumley came to see us for yet another television movie. We fell in love. I named my daughter after her.

More important still, the world now knows about our plight.

So faith will out...

CS: Sweet yet extremely poignant Roddy.

JM: Very good Roddy xx

PW: Well said Roddy and let's hope so. Must say Pongo's wife perhaps being a bit insulting to Pongo! Seriously very thoughtful and a great drawing. xx

BD: Delightful, Roddy.

MLM: Really liked this Roddy and as you know I feel the same having adopted two Orangatans a few years ago xxx - always love what you do s ml

FOOD FOR THOUGHT

Roddy Martine

ONCE upon a time, I had an alter ego called Julian Fraser. He came about in another century when I was editor of *Scottish Field* magazine and needed to recruit somebody to review Scottish restaurants.

I had previously employed the gourmet skills of the *Sutherland's Law* actor Iain Cuthbertson from Lockerbie, followed by the maverick Nicholas Fairbairn QC, MP, until I discovered that the latter, preoccupied with his legal and parliamentary peregrinations, would, instead of turning up in person, simply telephone the restaurants to ask what they had on their menus. When I discovered this from his perhaps rather too indiscreet secretary, I took the job in-house.

Becoming Julian Fraser was interesting. I was once talking to the manager of the very excellent Maryculter Hotel in Aberdeenshire who confided in me that the one person he truly dreaded turning up in his dining room was Julian. I nodded in sympathy.

On another occasion I asked the waiter in a restaurant in Helensburgh what the house wine was like? "I don't know," he replied. "But it's got a lovely label."

In my travels around Scotland – and I religiously covered my patch from the far north to deep south and from east to west and the Highlands and Islands – I would randomly pick a restaurant victim wherever I found myself. Dining on your own is never especially enjoyable except that I got into the habit of listening in on the conversations of those around me – illuminating stuff about family traumas, triumphs, sexual inadequacies, ambitions, disappointments, regrets and partisan religious and political hatreds. If you ever need a plot for a runaway best-selling novel go and dine somewhere on your own and listen in.

It was the early 1980s and a genuinely fascinating time to be a restaurant critic. Scotland was cautiously rediscovering its very own, long buried, neglected and much abused natural larder – Highland beef, venison, salmon, trout, lobster and langoustine, pheasant, grouse, raspberries, strawberries, tatties, beans and carrots and oats. Running up to its beatification as European City of Culture in 1990, and spurred on by the Struthers Advertising agency and Lord Provost Michael Kelly's ***"Glasgow's Miles Better"*** slogan, rough and ready Glasgow was undergoing a radical transformation.

No longer was eating out almost exclusively relegated to three and four star hotels or to Italian, Chinese or Indian emporiums although even the latter was being reinvented in Edinburgh by the arrival of that colourful duo, Tommy Miah and Wali Uddin from Bangladesh. I was a Patron of Tommy's Curry Club when he invited the junior health minister Edwina Currie to become its President. That was an odd coupling.

Such was Julian Fraser's influence in those days that he was also invited by the legendary soup queen Ena Baxter to sit on the then Scottish Tourist Board's fledgling Taste of Scotland Committee.

Meanwhile, in Glasgow, Ken McCulloch, a charismatic local boy, son of the Billy Cotton Band Show singer Kathy Kaye, opened up a string of trendy cocktail bars and restaurants – Charlie Parker's, Roganos, The Buttery, The Belfry and, latterly, One Devonshire Gardens. Next came the Ubiquitous Chip. Over the 1980s and 1990s, Glasgow exploded with the kind of fine dining experience hitherto unknown outside of the stately excess of The Malmaison Restaurant of The Central Hotel.

McCulloch's forays into Edinburgh, however, did not fair so well. The dress code of Charlie Parker's in George Street (chic. No jeans and woolly jumpers) sent the young punters, mostly well off university students, over the road to Maddogs.

What the Glasgow style did achieve, of course, was to fire up the next generation of East Coast restauranteurs, in particular that generous genius, James Thomson of The Witchery and The Tower in the Museum of Scotland, leading to his takeover of Prestonfield House. A platter of media driven celebrity chefs emerged – Nick Nairn, Gary Rhodes, Jamie Oliver, Mark Greenaway, Martin Wishart, Thomas Kitchen and the Roux Brothers.

Remember only three or four decades earlier, Edinburgh had boasted only one up-market licensed restaurant – L'Aperitif In Frederick Street - and it was closed on Sundays.

Seizing the opportunity, some of my greatest friends such as Clare Macdonald (whom I had hired as a cookery writer for *Scottish Field*), the late *Two Fat Ladies* Clarissa Dickson Wright, and the magnificent Pru Leith, launched themselves into writing best selling cookery books. Even I was called upon to write the forward to a lavishly illustrated volume – *Scottish Country Kitchen* by Ruth Shannon.

Nowadays, It is as if one out of every five television programmes on whatever Channel you choose to watch, is devoted to food in all of its manifest and magical interpretations. This is presumably to encourage the great couch potato audience to cook for themselves, although I doubt that many do.

And along with all of this faddish euphoria for excessive and often snobbish gourmet consumption (and the growing necessity to take out a bank loan to dine, out), there is the inevitable counter culture reaction – the seemingly unstoppable rise of the vegetarian and, horror of horrors, the vegan. Go to work on an egg plant, if you must.

You must always remember that you are what you eat.

But you should also be aware that there are consequences – obesity, allergies, diabetes, cholesterol.

I'm so much more alive now I'm gluten intolerant.

BD: Lovely, Roddy. Marvelously entertaining!

RM: Thanks Barbara x

CS: Yes, wonderful. I love the idea of the name Julian Fraser sending restaurateurs from East to West quaking in their boots.

ML: Roddy I loved it as always!!

CS: Excellent Roddy!

PW: Very interesting altogether Roddy and brought back memories for me. I worked the summer of 1975 at Loch Tummel Hotel when it was owned by the Skene's, Strathmiglo. I can't remember the manager Andrew's surname. It was very popular for its bar meals but also a good cordon bleu restaurant ahead of its time. The following year I worked at Peat Inn for a short while before taking up a summer job at Fort Augustus. David Wilson was an innovator not least in how he managed his staff team. All the team sat with David and his family for a full breakfast before the start of a long busy day. Nice to work with someone who looked out for his employees. David's kitchen was very calm and well organised as was the restaurant. I remember Glasgow having a very good restaurant scene early 80's and very occasionally a meal at Ubiquitous Chip.

CMS: Great history of Edinburgh restaurants- I know Tommy Miah well – always has an idea for selling our beer in return for large investment!

Marie-Louise Brulatour Mills

THE click of the knife on the block was rhythmic like a metronome. It suddenly stopped only to be substituted by the hiss of the garlic slices being thrown into the greased pan. The pungent perfume pervaded the small kitchen but even with the windows open the pungent odor remained until the tomato sauce smothered it. Soon the pasta boiled, drained and pasta sauce melded into a deep blue and white decorative bowl.

I scurried down the steep stone steps to place the steaming bowl placed on a mat of the glass table, a cluster of wisteria dangle down from the pergola above. The combination of the sweet and pungent fragrance married and soon my hungry guests devoured half its contents.

The guest list included the usual friends, an Irish Danish couple, a pair of squabbling Italians and a Gary Cooper look-alike, my partner. He collected an American acquaintance from a nearby hotel and unlike us, she wore a completely white couture pants suit. I knew this outfit would surely invite a splattering of tomato sauce, and soon did. Horrified, she stood up annoyed at me as if I did it, and my sympathy drained as soon as the bowl emptied.

"I suggest Gunter brings you immediately to the cleaners after lunch, as I don't know what takes out red sauce from linen," I said.

That prospect calmed her down but she remained agitated during the simple lunch while everyone else conversed.

The pop of the cork of the local white wine from Careganno silenced the guests until it was poured. The American refused it and demanded water, and stressed her need for ice.

"I have no ice. We don't use it. It's actually not good for the system," I said, and could immediately see her eyes narrowing to slits. I realised she probably was a reformed alcoholic and that set her apart once more.

Paddy the Irishman proposed conversation but while diffident, she finally revealed her outer life, focusing only on owning racehorses after the death of her father. This fact seemed to give licence to her superior attitude which aggravated most of the guests, including me. I thought to myself of the sign on new money; her pretention spelled it out most clearly.

"Deborah, I put my Stubbs place mats for you. Did you notice?"

"Oh yes, thanks," she said without an ounce of appreciation coming through her high voice.

I silently studied the stone wall with its disintergrating red bricks nearly swallowed by grasping ivy and dart back to looking up at the clear cloudless sky beyond the perfumed purple blossoms overhead.

Lunch was nearly finished but the imminent closure of the dry cleaners soon prompted the Gary Cooper look-alike and the American to excuse themselves and go upstairs and out of the front door. Lunch continued with more animated conversations but was long over when he returned near dinner time.

Life is indeed a platter of bitter and sweet.

Callum Stark

FOOD is one's constant friend. I'll challenge anyone who says otherwise. Chocolate will never argue, pasta never sulks, and cheese will most certainly never leave you.

Earlier this year I tried to eat solely vegan. I think the reason I failed – apart from decrepit moral fibre – is that it felt all too much like a funeral in my fridge every lunchtime, as I looked upon all that I couldn't eat. It was the culinary equivalent of having to bury every cherished friend or family member, being left with only one maiden aunt and a few dull people you used to sit next to in English class, for company.

It puts me in my mind of the artist Maggi Hambling, who had said that an artist must go to their work, and seek solace in it, be they tired, bored, happy or randy. I feel much the same about cooking. And obviously eating.

And yet, it is not obvious to many and there are those who eat only for sustenance and rarely for pleasure. I think now of my favourite aunt who would rather eat a pill than chow down and who, when last staying with us, ate my mum's banoffee pie for breakfast, lunch and dinner – it being the only food she really enjoys.

I think, too, of my elder brother who gets excited about a large T-bone steak, to satisfy his carnivorous urges and not much else.

For them, eating will be forever a verb and never a noun. They will eat but never be 'eaters', or gurgitators as A.A. Gill would say.

I am a gurgitator. And apparently I've always been so. In opposition to most children, I decried the bland and sought out the bold. I would bring heaving hunks of parmesan for my snack at nursery – larger than my three year old fist, and watch bemused as others unpeeled their baby bells. My parents would watch stunned waiters with amusement as I would order, and then proceed to make swift work of groaning bowls of mussels, the shells piling up until taller than I was.

A decade later I started cooking. Properly. It appeared to be - for one as greedy as I – the surest guarantee of having exactly what I wanted to eat, any time of day and night. I read cookbooks incessantly, often in bed, though very rarely cook from them. Mainly because I can't; people often think I am joking when I say I don't follow recipes because I'm bad with numbers. I'm not. I don't deal in precise food and to make something like a Victoria Sandwich requires me to muster every ounce of concentration and my scraped pass in National 5 maths. I'm much more comfortable in shloshes and handfuls than grams and ounces.

I'm not a bad cook though I'll admit that my tastes, at times, approach the grotesque. This is particularly so after a late night.

I've never felt the kebab to be a fitting finale to an evening and went through a phase of coming home and preparing toast spread thickly with butter then mayonnaise topped with parmesan or pecorino with at least three or four cloves of raw garlic on each slice.

My mum says I must be the only drunk that reaches for the garlic press come 4am. "I can't help it," I say. "What the gurgitator wants the gurgitator must have."

CMS: Brilliant Callum - won't mention the funeral in your fridge to Charlotte and Isabella but secretly agree!

JM Excellent piece Callum. See you soon.

RM: Skillful and beautifully written Callum. You are a magazine/ newspaper columnist already!

Pat Watson

FOOD - 'anything that nourishes or sustains'... For me 'food' is most enjoyable when combined with companionship, Alan, family and friends, everyone sat at a table sharing a meal.

The food I have eaten over the years has changed. I remember chicken being an absolute luxury when I was growing up. I never tasted turkey until the 70's. We ate plain fare, cereal, porridge, soup, mince always with vegetables and either lentils or oats added to spin out the meat, stews, Sunday roast – lamb, pork or beef, meat loaf, toad in the hole, potatoes, spam, jam sandwiches, orange squash, angel delight, milky puddings and on Friday overcooked poached fish...

I hated fish then. Pan bread never plain, my mother was very prejudiced re plain bread, wouldn't have it in the house. No idea why. She occasionally baked and we also had pancakes, scones, teacakes and fritters. We ate fresh veg from the garden and home-made jam. When my father had a glut of veg from the garden he would coat it in batter to encourage us all to eat it.

The first time I used garlic in my cooking was my first attempt at spaghetti bolognese for some friends in my first flat. The recipe included 1 clove of garlic but I had added a whole bulb... I thought it tasted grand although my friends did enquire about the amount of garlic!

One time shortly after moving to the west coast in the early 80's I visited the local supermarket. I enquired if they had some garlic anywhere and was offered garlic sausage. However this was also the era of vegetarianism, quiche, salads, baked potatoes, pizza, filled pancakes, Cranks and Henderson style cooking. As I remember it taking turns to share meals at each other's flats which inevitably turned into parties.

When my children came along some meat returned to my diet along with fish and chicken. Soup, salads, home baked bread and cakes, pancakes and scones. My father brought vegetables from his garden. Plain fare. When the children were fully fledged we found ourselves making tasty food like curry and the like and adding salt to the cooking.

Sadly this year I found myself eating alone for 3 months. Meals became a monotonous functional necessity. I found during this period of 'staying home' that the sorrow I experience having lost my husband last year intensified, often almost unbearable. It was so difficult to motivate myself to do anything very much at all.

I reminded myself how lucky I have been to have all those happy years sharing meals with family and friends. Somehow that made no difference. I have been very grateful for the distraction of this Decameron, for the interesting stories and chat. Thank you for inviting me along Andrew. It helped as did lovely phone chat and zoom chat with family and friends. Nothing can replace the sheer joy of being with people in the same space.

It is so lovely just now to have family home, albeit temporarily, and for food to be what it should be, a companionable highlight of the day, sharing stories, discussing current issues, chatting about people we know. It has reminded me that life will surely be normalised eventually.

I look forward to the time too I can visit with friends and them with me. 'Food' and 'food for thought' does sustain but so much more when shared in person especially with the people we love.

BD: Happy memories, Pat, of plain fare in my Dunfermline childhood. Lovely piece.

Andrew Brown

THE theme of food has been the most difficult subject for me so far and I have racked my brains about what to write. However, suddenly while cooking Sunday lunch today, I has a light bulb moment and realised, of course, that a picture is better than a thousand words. I therefore decided to produce a photo essay of my lunch today which though it may look a bit fraudulent is absolutely my usual Sunday product as Mark can testify to having eaten half of a similar chicken here (outdoors, of course) last Sunday, and most of the rest of you can rememebr from similar dinners before the lockdown and, as Dorothy said so poignantly, I cannot wait to host again here at Glen in the future.

My menu today was tomato basil and mozzarella salad in tribute to the Italian flag followed by herby chicken with roast potatoes and green beans followed by a cheese from Valvona & Crolla in Edinburgh, and washed down with Vernacchia dei Castelli dei Jesi and a delicious St Emilion, a special treat as it was reduced from £14 to £9 in Asda. Dessert will be those flat peaches in the bowl in the background if I ever get round to poaching them later in wine and gin with raspberries served with fresh cream, my version of Peach Melba.

So until we can all meet convivially to break bread together, bon apetit and, as my grandmother used to say, "you can't say you know somebody until they have eaten in your kitchen and you in theirs."

JM: Yes I had noticed. Have always said you know how to enjoy life!xX Potatoes look just right Hope we can come and enjoy some soon.

AB: Haven't poached peaches yet - in bed watching Terry Gilliam film Brazil with cheese and wine.

DJ: Excellent Andrew. I'm fond of the white wine you're enjoying.

Happier days before lockdown at The Glen

Dorothy Jackson

I'VE never had a particularly good relationship with food. I've been on some sort of diet since I was 21 – that's 44 years of watching or pretending to watch what I eat. I've always been a finicky eater – even in the 1950s and 1960s when money was not as plentiful I struggled to enjoy a wide range of foods.

Mind you, when I think back, some of the foods that I was shunning were liver, kidney, tongue, Cod's roe, soused herring, potted hough and tripe. Now, some of those foods are considered delicacies. My mother was not fond of most of these foods but my dad embraced them all with relish.

I vividly remember the first time I ate frozen food. My cousin and I visited my maiden aunt on a Saturday and were allowed to choose any foods we wished for dinner. As my aunt did not have a family to feed, she could afford these luxuries. Foods such as oven chips, rissoles and fish. We also often had Lyons cupcakes, orange and lemon, We halved them so we could have a bit each.

When on holiday as a child and at the seaside, my father would enjoy cockles and mussels from stalls along the promenade. I preferred the hot mini doughnuts that were also available. During my two week summer holiday with my parents, I was allowed one Knickerbocker Glory.

I so looked forward to it and it never failed to please. One time whilst on holiday, my mother went to get her hair done at the hairdressers (it was quite common to do that in the 1960s) and my father and I went to a cafe to have the aforementioned Knickerbocker Glory.

I should say that my mother was a keen knitter and it was tradition for her to knit us all a new Aran sweater for our holiday. My father was sporting a cream one – and decided at the end of his ice cream that he would up-end the dish to get the last bit out of it. Of course, the strawberry, and some ice cream that was at the very bottom, came rushing out all over the new sweater. Not only that but all the other customers in the cafe seemed to have seen what had happened and were trying not to laugh. As was I! Needless to say my mother was not happy.

My primary school was in the main street in Wishaw (now a Lidl's) and depending on the wind direction, we knew what King's Sweet Factory was manufacturing by the smell.

Strong smells like mint for their Imperials and also spices such as cloves and cinnamon for their Oddfellows and Aromatics. On a Saturday, I was allowed 2ozs of Seaside Donkeys. They also manufactured Cherry Lips that I was not fond of but my cousin loved. Sweet and chocolate rationing didn't finish until 1953 and I think my generation were given lots of these because our parents had been denied it for so long.

I recently read Deborah Orr's autobiography *Motherwell* and recognised so much of the detail in this book. Although younger than me, I did know a couple of the people she remembered fondly in her book. She mentioned a local obstetrician called Dr Grieve who had a strong regime with the mothers under his care. Indeed, his philosophy was part of a study by the Universities of Edinburgh and Southampton where a group called the 'Motherwell Babies' were studied because Dr Grieve had extensive records of the diets of the women under his care in the 1950s and 1960s, I don't think my mother was looked after by him but she often quoted him when suggesting that corned beef was good for you and also that even Dr Grieve allowed the odd boiled sweet. I think his diet might have verged on a forerunner of the Atkins Diet.

One of my favourite books is *Toast* by Nigel Slater. It has parts that made me laugh out loud. I highly recommend it. In a review of the book by Matthew Fort for *The Observer,* he states that the 'story' begins with burnt toast and ends with profiteroles and hot chocolate. My son Andrew says he will always remember me by the smell of burnt toast, as I do have a tendency to burn toast. Nigel Slater's memoir is not just an autobiography but also an homage to his love of food.

When I was a student in Glasgow in the 1970s, I was introduced to one of my favourite foods – a Glasgow Curry. In those days we frequented restaurants in the city centre and also on Gibson Street. The favourite there was The Shish Mahal.

I have a cook book somewhere among the many cook books I own (but just look at). I'm sure many people do that. There was also the phenomenon of the indescribables – or jaggy pakora.

Pakora came to Glasgow with the wave of settlers from the Punjab after Indian independence. The first Curry Shop in Glasgow opened in 1954 and by the time I was in Glasgow they were well established.

My friend's son, who lives in Sevenoaks, laments the fact that he can't buy pakora there. I saw a comment in an article on-line where the author – an Expat called Audrey Gillan, is amused by the statement,"The idea of selling a giant plateful of vegetables to Glaswegians who would never order vegetables, is remarkable." They are deep fried though!

Curry houses such as Shenaz and The Little Curry Shop are very popular in Glasgow. My absolute favourite is Mother India's Cafe – just opposite Kelvingrove Art Gallery and Museum. I like the small restaurant which serves tapas sized dishes. The décor is great too.

I do enjoy the social aspects of food very much. I love the feeling of sharing and the camaraderie around a table. I like eating outside (I suppose because this is a rare occasion in Scotland). This year has been an exception and we've thoroughly enjoyed sitting in the gazebo at the top of the garden. I've been very grateful that the weather has been good. We have been given a present of a lovely big barbecue but, as it's in Aviemore, we can't use it. I miss my visits to Aviemore and Glen. I'm looking forward to seeing everyone and sharing some food,

PW: Dorothy, your story is fabulous, I am there. I like looking at cook books too. As for cooking though rarely consult a cook book, enough said!! xx

PW: My late neighbour of some 20 years told me a good story of how when newly married her husband spent a night at the pub with his pals. She decided to feed him tripe! X

BD: Thank you, Dorothy.

DJ: Tripe and onions! My friend on her first visit to her now husband's family was given oxtail! Again, now, probably a delicacy.

PW: Absolutely Dorothy, had oxtail once many years ago in another lifetime. The Ardross farm shop by Elie sells quail's eggs, a lovely treat which my grandchildren particularly enjoy. Looking forward to being able to visit there again.

PW: We are very lucky to have a very good network of farms distributing locally produced food in Fife. Pittormie Farm has been bringing me food since lockdown. So grateful for their support and currently enjoying their strawberries.

JM: Also looking forward the sharing food and drink with everyone, a very important part of life. Dorothy ,/Mother India is one of our favourite restaurants in Glasgow. Its our usual haunt when we go over to Visit Thomas. We also have the cookbook! X

DJ: I'm so looking forward to seeing everyone - in the flesh. X

CS: Wonderful piece Dorothy - you, Jessie and I can form a Mother India fan club, I love it. Though I go to the Edinburgh one a lot more than the one in Glasgow.

Jonathan Gibbs

A GARDEN FEAST. Oil on wood panel 24 X 40cm.

A late post to be read at any time, with apologies. Here is a recent painting that explored the ideas of vessels, tables, domesticity, and the still life.

These are recurrent themes, since art college times, in drawing, painting & printmaking, This painting is currently exhibited at the Moncrieff Bray Gallery, Sussex.

On a more specific note, in 1986, I went to a meeting in Jeffrey Street, in Edinburgh, in a top floor flat. This was the Canongate Publishing office and where Stephanie Wolfe Murray also lived, I think. From that meeting I illustrated Tom Pow's first collection of poetry, *Rough Seas*.

At that time Tom was a school teacher in Dumfries, where I visited to make research drawings to inform my illustrations. That book led to *A Flavour of France* by Odette Murray, which is a book all about food in Scotland.

As an illustrator, I have made many wood engravings about food. From my point of view, these are always still-lives. I have a great admiration of Elizabeth David's books, both for the literature and pictures. These artists were Adrian Daintrey and John Minton. Minton's finest work, I believe.

Wood Engravings for Canongate: ORANGES DU SOLEIL

Wood engraving 10 x 12.5cm.

APRON, CREPES, POTAGE.

Other significant figures are Jane Grigson, Dorothy Hartley, with various other food critics in the *Sunday Times Guardian, Scotsman* and *Telegraph.* A good art editor will choose the most appropriate illustrator to suit the text. But when I taught illustration and did projects about food, we looked at Manet, Bonnard, Matisse as well as sculpture, film and printmaking.

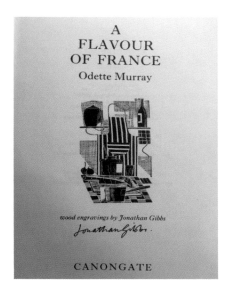

At Canongate, I have to mention Neville Moir, as well as Stephanie Wolfe Murray and the great James Hutcheson who continues to make beautiful cover designs for all sorts of books. He designed *Rough Seas*, *A Flavour of France*, *The Moth Trap* and *Reading the Bones* by Janet Paisley. Hutcheson is a consummate artist in the world of print and painting.

CS: Amazing Johnny! Particularly your woodcuts. I love Elizabeth David too and it's unimaginable to think of her books unaccompanied by John Minton's drawings.

CMS: That's wonderful- Stephanie was responsible for putting so many people together - I still can't believe she's no longer here

DJ: Very interesting Johnny! I have a couple of the Folio Society editions of Elizabeth David. Andrew (my son) bought me them.

Catherine Maxwell Stuart

Whole Food Paradise

THE first experience I had of Neal's Yard was in the mid-1970s. I remember visiting my uncle's new shop – The Wholefood Warehouse. He had recently purchased a building in a very run down part of London – Covent Garden, and the Yard consisted of several rat infested warehouses that served the old fruit and veg market.

The shop was on the ground floor with the first floor used as a packing room and he had created a huge open-plan flat for himself on the top floor with a roof garden. It was designed like a ship with tiny porthole windows and a toilet with a glass cistern that was filled with gold fish who must have had a disorientating life as the water filled and emptied whenever the toilet was flushed.

When I was about 15 I was allowed to go and spend a few weeks working there in the summer. It was quite an experience. By this time, my uncle, Nicholas, had purchased two other buildings in the yard and was setting up co-operatives to form a bakery, dairy and apothecary. The night I arrived, Randolph and Anita who were running the dairy were moving in and we spent many hours unloading equipment, taking delivery of cheeses from Caerphilly to Orkney, never seen before in London. Best of all, they began to make ice cream and the fresh smell of milk and cheese used to waft out of the door and into the yard.

Next door, the bakery was making incredibly wholesome bread. Those loaves that weighed a stone and provided untold roughage were very popular at the time and their sandwiches were quite a feat to eat - bursting with egg mayonnaise, cress and sprouting seeds in a large seeded giant of a bun. The smell of freshly baked bread often exceeded the actual product.

My job was in the packing department where we mixed and filled large bags of muesli. The smells were nourishing in themselves – a warm mix of flour, oats, raisins and nuts. I sat next to a lovely pregnant Danish girl whom I later found out was carrying my uncle's baby. We packed and weighed bags then sent them down a chute into the shop.

When deliveries were unloaded they were hoisted to the first floor by a human pulley. One person would attach the load, a second would jump out of the window holding the rope coming down from the pulley, while the third would haul in the load. It was hard work and things were always going wrong but Nicholas was passionate about his low tech innovations.

He had other unusual and innovative practices in the warehouse. Food was priced according to how much work had been put into packing it, so grains and beans were cheap while sticky items like dates and prunes in small packs were pricey.

The Yard started to become a meeting place and my uncle planted trees in large oil drums with tables so people would hang out at lunchtime surrounded by delicious food and smells issuing from every doorway.

Just around the corner was the Monmouth Street Coffee House, another of my uncle's ventures. He realised there was nowhere near you could buy ground coffee from freshly roasted beans in London so the coffee house was born and it was in the attic flat above the shop that I ended up living as a student in the '80s.

By this time, the Yard had got so successful the original businesses had grown and expanded. Any thoughts of co-operatives were forgotten and eventually they all left the yard with the exception of the original Neals yard Apothecary, which is still there today. My uncle became deeply disillusioned and felt his input and generosity to the start ups had been unappreciated. He moved on to promoting other ideas such as experimenting with Ecstacy and writing a book about its benefits.

By the late '90's, the Yard had changed beyond all recognition. Carluccios eventually took over the bakery, a cheap juice bar inhabited the old dairy and worse still, the whole food warehouse was bought by Holland and Barrett and returned to a conventional style health food shop.

However, I like to remember that magical yard when I lived there with the constant aroma of roasted coffee, delicious cheeses and yoghurts for lunch and dining out at our favourite vegetarian restaurant, Food for Thought, just around the corner for no more than a fiver. My own foodie paradise!

DJ: I love your memories Catherine. I order coffee from the Monmouth Street Coffee Shop. I once bought some at Borough Market and put it in a bag which I wore as a messenger bag. I was followed round London with this fabulous smell! Every time I moved I got a whiff!! 😊 😊

AB: Marvelous memories I remember going there in the eighties and having those delicious looking but inedible sandwiches I knew it was owned by your uncle the Timothy Leary of England but didn't know you had worked there

RM: Super Marie Louise and Catherine. These should be published.

JM: I was at the Central School of Art just down the road, finally leaving in 1976 and have happy memories of Neals Yard . It must have been just when they were starting out. Was your uncle called Neal?

CMS: No, he was Nicholas - Thomas Neale was given the yard in 1690 by William III who created the Seven Dials area.

BD: Catherine, I was one of those who refilled my huge jars at Neal's Yard! Living in Clapham, I just whizzed up in my mini clubman and restocked. The apple juice concentrate was delicious!!! X

Neals Yard in London

Mark Muller Stuart – Food for Thought

WHEN Dorothy selected food it immediately conjured up images of being served lunch and Pinot Noir in the little French restaurant in Broughton Street in Edinburgh – of meeting the two Marks for afternoon snacks in the Bombay Parsi- inspired Cafe Dishoom – of summer dinners with Michael and Catherine and the family in the square of the medieval hill top town of Cupramonta in La Marcha in Italy – of soirees of salads with Tim Phillips in Martha's Vinyard – and of Wiener schnitzel dinners with Billy and Dorothy in Andrew's 19th century 'Tardis' at Glen. How cruel of Dorothy to invoke such images during lockdown.

But then I forced myself to think of less mouth-watering encounters with food. Of being forced to eat a rooster's claw after not eating for 24 hours, aged 19, moneyless, as I made my way from Penang to Singapore on a packed bus to pick up a credit card – it was the only thing I could afford.

Of having to eat, as the honoured guest of a tribal chief in Oman, the fatted hump of a young camel which had been cooked and placed whole on a huge silver plate in the desert, all gristle.

Of having to eat a green coloured egg offered up to me by some Kurdish women whose homes had just been burned by the Turkish military in the summer of 1994. They had lost some of their young menfolk under a tank and had nothing to eat but yet they still gave us food.

As dusk dimmed the effect of the scorching sun, the remaining men appeared from the fields. "It's a miracle you have come," one said as I made my speech while staring at my western colleagues as each one raced to take the healthy-looking eggs for themselves. I couldn't refuse the last green one for fear of dishonouring the villagers. I later spent 2 weeks holed up in a small hotel retching from food poisoning and ruminating on the quality of western solidarity and honour.

Of having to eat the most watery forlorn piece of lamb I have ever seen after passing through 35 check-points to get to rebel-held Benghazi during the Arab Spring. 'Gaddafi had always hated Benghazi', the waiter explained. 'He left us with nothing.'

However, he left me with the memory of it which Dorothy has now made me relive in order to banish from my mind all those wonderful earlier images of food and friends, the loss of which must surely rank as one of the greatest downsides of lockdown.

RM: Marvelous Mark

MM: And I should have added of the wonderful dinners had at Beyond Borders in the enchanting dinning rooms and pavilions of Traquair!

DJ: We're planning a schnitzel party as soon lockdown's over!

Kurdish women in their burnt out home in South East Turkey in 1993.

TRANSITION

Catherine Maxwell Stuart

AS women we live in a state of constant transition. From childhood to puberty, menstruation to motherhood and then the menopause. There never seems to be a break. The constant emotional upheavals that go with physical changes are exhausting but can come with rewards.

Becoming a mother is undoubtedly the biggest transition most women ever make and it certainly was for me.

As a young woman I remember being incredibly focused on avoiding motherhood. I felt absolutely no inclination to mother any child. I was slightly repulsed by babies, particularly the smell, the noise, the dribbling. I was quite astounded that women so easily fell into this trap from which you could never be released.

Yet there was a feeling of inevitability that it was going to happen sometime and by the time I was in my later twenties and just married, of course, it did.

Even when I fell pregnant I spent the whole of my pregnancy panicking I wouldn't bond with my baby. It took me completely by surprise that when Isabella finally arrived and I looked my baby in the face, I fell utterly and completely in love. I literally couldn't keep my eyes off her. She was part of me yet entirely independent. I was also terrified as I didn't have a clue how to "be a mother."

That night I remember lying in a hospital bed with the baby in a cot beside me trying to sleep. When she woke, crying, I instinctively rang the bell for the nurse.

The woman who whipped the curtain aside was of the battle-axe variety. When I nervously told her the baby was crying, she said furiously," There are only three reasons why babies cry. They are hungry; they need their nappy changed, or they want a cuddle," and she flounced off before I had a chance to say I wasn't sure how to do any of these things.

Strangely it was Mark who came to the rescue the next day. He came to visit us in hospital and as he had a much younger brother, he was adept at nappy changing and gave me a quick lesson. Even my mother was quite impressed.

Having a baby has been described as if you are entering a room in your house that you never knew existed. It is true that being a mother began to feel like the most natural thing in the world on good days and the most exhausting, frightening and paralysing experience on others.

My husband John was very ill when Isabella arrived and no doubt the unsettled background of her first few months affected her. She could cry for hours on end and I could do nothing to stop her. It put into sharp focus how quickly you stop thinking about yourself and every waking hour is devoted to pacifying the new tiny tyrant that suddenly and completely fills your life.

A year or two in and there was a general adjustment to this new state of motherhood and a growing confidence in my ability to care for the growing child.

By the time the second, Louis, arrived on a Borders' hillside (we didn't quite make it to the hospital) two and a half years later, I found myself with two ambulance men and Mark, all of whom had never been present at a birth.

As they were focused on driving as fast as possible to the hospital, I knew I was going to have to take control of the events. I knew now exactly what was happening.

I remember screaming, "Just stop the f***** ambulance, I'm giving birth NOW. A few minutes after we stopped, Louis was born.

Having two children was a period of feeling you are creating a family and finding an ability to be more relaxed as a mother. Charlotte's arrival (at home, thankfully), was calm, the only drama was its speed. She popped into the world in less than an hour.

The most fantastic reward of all is to watch the children's' transitions from screaming toddler, divinely adorable boy and girls to monosyllabic teenagers and now, surprisingly mature young adults.

Yes, I fell well and truly into the trap of motherhood and enjoying every moment.

DJ: So well said Catherine. I was in a brand new unit that had just opened. I had taught a number of the nurses and auxiliaries and was also with some ex pupils who were having babies and were largely much more adept than I was at looking after their babies. They helped me! Tables had happily turned. I welcomed their help. I'm still in touch with some of them. X

MLM: Catherine a hard subject to write about so beautifully explained observed and felt. Thank you for sharing what are intimate feelings 🙏🐘🤱♡ml

PW: Catherine, you describe the whole experience beautifully. All too true. XX

RM: Circle of life Catherine. Great. x

Mark Muller Stuart

TRANSITION we are told is the process or period of changing from one state or condition to another. Yet, what I find most fascinating about transition are those "constants" or "permanences" that accompany or remain with us as we go through such a process or period of change – such as consciousness, character, values, friends and our intuitive capacity to narrate and curate the process of change itself.

For I have been lucky enough to have felt such constants throughout all of the transitions that have affected my life. Whether such constants be real, imagined or conceived does not matter. What matters is their ability to give historical shape, meaning, purpose and hope to life.

That I am the product of profound transitions can be in no doubt. It was as a consequence of political transition that my father lost his father aged 12 during Partition in India in 1947, after the British imposed a political, religious and ethnic transition on an unsuspecting populous in an attempt to create two states from one complex country in just six weeks, having ruled over the place for 200 years.

As the midnight hour chimed on 15 August 1948, and Mountbatten's Raj disappeared like rats into the night, the British announced the line of partition leading to political outcry, chaos on the streets, the emergency transfer of two populations and the deaths of millions, including my grandfather.

It was a decision that would take my father onto the streets of Delhi, then to Canada into exile, before settling in London aged 19, where he would meet my mother.

She in turn was the product of another partition and transition – of a divided Germany and its journey from Nazi totalitarianism to European democracy and Soviet authoritarianism.

My Mother's family property was lucky enough to fall on the democratic side of the fence yet quite remarkably, she decided, aged just 16 years, to escape the social conservatism of the Black Forest in 1957 to elope with herself to Britain despite its residual hostility towards Germans.

Both my parents were Talismans for a new world as they enthusiastically embraced the freedoms that the late 'fities and 'sixties had to offer.

Despite being buffeted by social and political transition, a global thread and an inner logic seemed to run through their lives. Our house in London became a place of political debate and dance. This included my godfather who interestingly after reading Pat's contribution, I should record was the guy who as No 2 of the Greater London Council in the early 1980s, put the unemployment figures onto the GLC building to remind Thatcher's Parliament and Britain about the cost of her own form of transition for the country.

Yet for all the freedom of post-war Britain, I can still recall as a child in the 1970s the frightened look on my German grandmother's face as she beckoned my mother to close the windows of our London home on a baking summer's day in 1976 for fear of others overhearing what was being said. The experiences of the 1930s had never left her.

Terror – and the loss of it – often accompany and animate political and personal transition. Aged 14, I became so tired of being scared of the school bully I decided to walk up to 'Boner' (he was 6 foot and 2 inches tall) in the middle of the school playground and shout "So Boner, how come you're such a big hit with the girls?"

The whole playground burst into laughter. Boner immediately grabbed me by the throat but as he did, I caught the unmistakable glimpse of fear and humiliation in his eye. He bounced me on the top of my head but later came to offer me a deal whereby he would not hit me if I stopped the jokes. I said I would if he laid off all my friends too.

I often thought of Boner during the revolutions of 1989 and the Arab Spring when ordinary people somehow found the strength to rise up against oppression despite unbelievable odds. Boner taught me a lesson in life – that although social orders are seemingly made up of impregnable institutions and rules – underneath they are all staffed by individuals moving through time with their own desires and concerns.

From that moment on I moved through life in a different way. Roosevelt was right – the only thing to fear is fear itself. It is why Andrew has been able to lead the life he has lived.

Looking back now, my whole seems to have been dominated by transition – from my family origins to my professional work in courts and conflicted zones (where life chances regularly turned on a dime) on to my Dick Wittington-like reverse relocation from the City of London to the wilds of the Scottish Borders.

But throughout these twists and turns I have been lucky enough to be accompanied by friends – like Catherine – like Andrew – who have shared my successes and failures.

These constants are critical to human life. The sharing of memories and human spaces with others infuses seemingly inhuman transitions with meaning and hope despite the human capacity for evil.

Many find similar sustenance and solace in the making of Art and the recording of History. Indeed, it is often remarked that great culture is predominantly generated through times of acute political, social and personal transitions and upheavals.

But what is it that makes us attempt to encapsulate such experiences?

To my mind it is because we retain a form of consciousness that does not just simply 'clock' our environment as we transition through it but actively seeks out social meaning and human solidarity as we do so.

That is why the arc of history points in favour of justice. It is also why we find the lockdown so painful.

Human consciousness does not simply connect past experience to future lives. It allows for conscious decisions and active judgements about it. This form of consciousness is unique to humanity and is what generates value.

It is why we set up courts to punish transgressive behaviour. It underpins the self-evident truths upon which the claim to inalienable rights is based – namely a capacity for human dignity and solidarity based upon our moral ability to not only choose but also judge and forgive.

Which leads me to Traquair.

In travelling through this restless, rootless and transitional world, it has been my great luck and privilege to have happened upon Traquair. Who knows whether it was destiny or chance which brought me here?

Me thinks it was neither but a receptiveness to love and friendship of others. What is extraordinary, however, is not just how this House has physically managed to withstand all the trials and tribulations of the great transition of Scottish and British political religious and social history, it is how it has housed a single family throughout that time who – for whatever reason – remained committed to particular bonds of human association – be they religious, political or personal – without fear or favour.

It matters not whether the bonds they nurtured triumphed over other associations. What matters is that they were continually valued, recognised, kept and nurtured throughout good and bad times for better or worse. They became constants in the human story which gave sustenance to the next generation. All of this says something about the power of the human spirit in times of transition.

The Gates of Traquair stand today not simply as an emblem of lost causes but as a testament to and for all those who fought for transitions that failed to occur. Traquair, whose motto is *Judge Nought*, is not just a physical monument to human memory, it is a place of sancturay and refuge.

As such, it has become another wonderful constant in my life. It is why I felt able to set up Beyond Borders there, which now helps others from around the world to share experiences and make sense of their own transitions.

The family history of Traquair has now been eloquently added to by Catherine in *Decameron* as we all seek to document our reaction to the current transition we are living through.

So – as we near the end of *Decameron* – and attempt to emerge from the lockdown of what will surely become known as the great Pandemic of 2020 – let us raise a glass to ourselves for deciding to participate in *Decameron*.

For through it – and the gift of human consciousness – given miraculously to us by the Universe – we have recorded our own little bit of history and renewed the bonds of human friendship and solidarity.

MLM: Mark loved your piece...again and I raise a glass to all and to you and your fine and sensitive writing.

PW: Interesting read Mark. Let's hope we are not returned to lockdown by August!

Marie Louise Brulatour Mills

THE Miraculous medal dangled from the long blue cord around my neck, flirting as it flickered on the chrome toaster. My twelve-year old face swelled and distorted its reflection expanding my thin features and emphasising the ruler straight bangs with a tightly curled pageboy.

I sat in a straight-backed chair, an uncomfortable one as neither it nor I had padding. I consistently squirmed from that daily discomfort each morning.

"Can I please have an English muffin?" I asked. The muffins soon popped up, were soon buttered and Elizabeth's long tapered fingers held the square plate with raised animal forms racing around its border and placed it on the kitchen table. I ran my fingers around the strange animals that circled the rim.

"What are they Elizabeth?" I asked.

"They are imagined animals, someone's creation," she said after she sat down with a freshly brewed coffee with its bewitching aroma that lingers in my memory and continues to be my morning ritual. She carefully and somehow accurately smeared her bright red lipstick on her lips and put on her knobby red wool coat before we started our daily walk to school.

At Park Avenue and 79th Street, we crossed the busy wide street that links the East and West sides of Manhattan and came to a small building with animal's statues lurking on its roof.

"These look like the animals on the plates," I said, staring at the same shapes of those unidentifiable animals.

"Yes, they are both griffons and gargoyles," she she said as she released our gloved hands to point to the decorative spout nearly hidden by the strange animal's face above it.

Now more mythical creatures jumped from those plates to living, and matured in my head until the moment I questioned their validity but also those of the saints studied so rigorously in Catholic schools. Were they like the mythological beasts, not exactly real but based on something true? Were they too 'someone's creation"? Did that dangling medal represent reality or an idea, or both?

The small private home with the gargoyles became an Embassy before it was knocked down. Would the saints have such a fate? After all, Saint Christopher and Saint Philomena disappeared just like the neo-gothic buildings.

My old medal remains in the bottom drawer, but I thumb through Medieval manuscripts, and listen to early music imagining the world of imaginary beast with delight.

RM: I love your world of gargoyles and mythical beasts Marie Louise. Very NY.x

CS: Yes – it's wonderful ML!

Callum Stark

THE past few months have been nothing if not ones of transition; each week a positive milfoil of unprecedented experience.

I felt this particularly keenly turning eighteen in quarantine only a few days into lockdown. Despite this coming of age – a day of such cultural and legal significance – I felt younger not older.

Since at least the age of eleven, though arguably since I learned to walk at nine months, I have led a life largely independent of my family; a semi-detached kind of youth. In a matter of days that independence, so important to my sense of self, was all but dissolved. For the first time in a long time I had very little outside the home to call mine and mine alone.

Days before my birthday I had prematurely left school – yet another supposedly significant milestone that when it came reeked of anti-climax. I thought it would feel like the toppling of a great dictator. It had always seemed an immense buffer to the way I wished to live my life; irritating, infantilised punctuation to all that happened elsewhere. So, think of my surprise that, when it did come, I was not free as a bird but transferred merely to a different – more comfortable – cage.

Yet – despite having written 209 words on the subject – I don't think it is helpful to dwell on these things. Transitions are, by nature, temporary. Indeed, as the lockdown has lifted, I feel I have experienced a kind of adolescence in vitro.

And one thing that has emerged from all this is that with any transition it is almost always better to sway with the wind, like a palm tree, rather than against and snap.

MM: Well done Callum. I hazard a guess Callum that your memories of this Spring will become more aromatic and meaningful as the years go by just like a good wine should. Can you imagine writing a Decameron in 50 years when we will all be gone!

Jessie Ann Mathew

   DURING this lockdown and sticking to the local rule, we have been going down to our local burn Keith Water. I have been trying to capture the trees and surrounding landscape.

   Of course, in the beginning there were no leaves and now you cannot see the branches (much more difficult!).

Beautiful colours in the Spring.

Now the greens are a much more unified colour and shapes harder to define.

CS: Wonderful Jessie – and you'll know what Virginia Woolf said of literature vs art – probably in reference to Vanessa. "Words are an impure medium, better to have been born in the silent kingdom of paint."

Andrew Brown

ALTHOUGH I might have brushed past them in a gay bar or night club, I had never really met or talked to a transvestite or transsexual until around fifteen years ago when a London friend introduced me to a louche semi-illegal nightclub in Limehouse called Stunners. It was run by a former antique and veteran car dealer originally christened Peter but now named Jane. Over a few months I got to know her and her favourite clientele well and it was a revelation to me to become intimate with these brave transvestites, drag queens and transsexuals and hear their often heartbreaking stories of ridicule and rejection from former friends and families, especially from those committed souls who were engaged in the full transition from male to female.

I painted Jane's portrait several times, first in her home surprisingly modestly dressed in sweater, skirt and sandals, and later more typically in the club in a fabulous feather coat and hat like a coster queen or Edwardian dowager duchess.

She encouraged me to become a semi-official recorder of the club since photography was not allowed to protect the identity of the clientele who were prominent professionals and often happily married.

I set up a studio in the 'Ladies' changing room and recorded the less timid clients in all their glory. Jane likened our relationship to that of Toulouse Lautrec and La Goulie at the Parisian Follies or, like Francis Bacon and Muriel Belcher at the colony club in London's Soho.

It was a privileged insight into an exotic twilight world of tawdry glamour where I was completely accepted despite my personal lack of interest in dragging myself up. Indeed, when a new door person denied me entrance one night because I was neither in drag or fetish gear, Jane swooped down like a great bird and pulled me in, declaiming, "Tartan and tweed are Andrew's drag, dear."

Roddy Martine

"JE suis le roi des choses transitoires," boasted Compte Robert de Montesquiou (1855-1922), poet, essayist, cat loving aesthete and confidant of Marcel Proust, Samuel-Jean Pozzi and James McNeil Whistler.

It was Montesquieu upon whom Proust modelled his eminence gris, the magnificent Baron de Charlus of À *la recherche du temps perdu* but I'm still inclined to think of them as an unlikely foursome. The insomniac Proust, writing through the night in his cork lined bedroom, was certainly obsessed with transition. Pozzi, preserved for posterity in a red coat by John Singer Sergent in the National Portrait Gallery, was shot by the cuckolded husband of a woman he had seduced, and while Whistler, grumpy at the best of times, sued the obsessive art critic John Ruskin for libelling his craft, he was to immortalise his dear little old widowed mother in black and white. Love is rare, life is strange, nothing lasts, people change. All gone in a blink.

I have to admit that I'm still not quite sure where I am going with this but it does strike me that as we all grow older and totter towards the tomb, some of us are increasingly inclined to be far more passionate about the past than the future. I don't have a problem with that. At least I know the chapter endings.

As an editor, publisher and columnist, as opposed to journalist, I have witnessed the transition from hot metal printing to Xerography and Web Offset; from manual typewriter to those funny electric golf ball contraptions. Then came the Internet, Lord Sugar's wretched Amstrad (I had one) with floppy discs, IBM, iPads and iPods, Apple, Blackberries, mobile phones which doubled as cameras, digital pictures, broadband, super broadband, Facebook, Twitter, Texting, Skype, Face Time and Zoom.

Newspaper copy takers, begone. Readers and subs, begone. Bring on the pdf. Ignore the grammar; don't bother about the spelling. Publish with Amazon. Buy a Kindle. I'm not going out any more, I just want to google.

I so vividly remember my first day with the *Sunday Times* at Kinning Park in Glasgow in 1991 and being shown to my desk.

"That's your screen," I was told.

I can recall staring at the keyboard in horror. I'd never used Microsoft Windows before but then the words of my old boss Maurice Hedges at Forth Publishing came to the rescue. "Roddy, when I ask you to fly a helicopter, I don't give a damn if you can fly a helicopter or not. When I ask you if you can fly a helicopter and you can't, I expect you to find out how to do so."

I smiled at the pretty girl at the adjoining desk and confessed," This system is a little different to the one I'm used to."

"Oh, don't worry. I'll show you how," she responded. And she did.

When we reached the year 2000, the National Museum of Scotland curated a personality-driven 20th century exhibition on its top floor and invited me to submit a single item that had changed my life. Tony Blair, as a Fettes schoolboy, had dreamed of becoming a rock star and so produced an electric guitar; Magnus Linklater donated his father's First World War army helmet from the trenches with a dent in it caused by shrapnel. Kirsty Wark selected an expensive car, a BMW or was it a Triumph Spitfire? I don't remember.

I chose a lap top word processor and for the ensuing year, museum visitors shared the enviable treat of seeing my face on its screen.

To keep myself occupied over this recent Corona-virus lockdown period, I have been sorting through some thirty albums of old photographs kept in a trunk – an exceedingly large trunk. A recent discovery has been that I am able to create printed photo books on-line and since I have my own scanner, and plenty of time, I have been systematically digitising and d.p.i. enhancing the transitory nature of my life.

So who is that bespectacled teenage geek, so skinny you couldn't see him sideways?; that raunchy contact lensed Warren Beattie look-alike (I wish) in the plum velvet frock coat from the early 'seventies disco scene?; that crumpled magazine editor of the 'eighties and 'nineties whom the late, great Harpers & Queen editor Ann Barr singled out as the only Sloane Ranger in Scotland?; that self-employed media hack of the 'naughties, and that neurotic, conscious of running-out-of-time, grey haired survivor of the sweet and twenty 'twenties? All of those caricatures are to be found in those albums, several mercifully out-of-focus.

Early on in my career. my editor-in-chief Eric Baird recommended that in the absence of a staff photographer, I should always carry a camera to capture those inevitable fleeting moments that would never again repeat themselves. Despite my being a card carrying member of the NUJ (which in those days actively discouraged print journalists from using cameras), I have followed his advice ever since.

The one good thing about being behind a camera is that you accumulate thousands of photographs of other people and only a selective few of yourself.

But those that I have kept irrevocably bookmark my life – kissing the hand of Katie Boyle (does anybody nowadays remember Katie Boyle?); standing on the roof of the World Trade Centre a decade before 9/11; at the Brandenburg Gate just after the Berlin Wall was demolished; at an award ceremony on the steps of the State Capitol in Washington (now only accessible for the inauguration of American presidents); shaking hands with Ronald Reagan at, curiously enough, Auchterarder House; taking tea with Dame Barbara Cartland in Helmsdale; discussing Scottish country dancing with Rudolph Nureyev in Paris, and my goddaughter Evie sitting on my shoulders to watch the 2012 Olympic torch pass through Exeter.

With the exception of Evie, whom I see often, what became of all those wonderful characters? Where did all the good times go, all the flowers and the wine? What does it matter? Who cares? Wha's like us? Damn few an' they're a' died.

Let's face it, at the end of the day we are all, each and every one of us, kings and queens of transitory things.

BD: Roddy, such a wonderful read, as ever. And yes, I remember Katie Boyle well. She once said she always found a parking space in the West End because she said a Hail Mary for one. It immediately appeared! Xx

RM: Thanks Barbara. All memories xx

CS: Brilliant as well as prompt as always Roddy! I also don't know if I've ever seen a laptop that big before - showing my age or rather youth

RM: In an age before small became beautiful

JM: Lovely Roddy. Great laptop pic! Xx

DJ: Excellent Roddy! X

CMS: What a life rich in experiences!

RM: And many more to come I hope Catherine xxx

PW: Your reflective contribution moving and interesting Roddy. Working with photos brings back so many memories I find and you do sound to have a treasure trove of them. xx

Jonathan Gibbs – Transition

OXFORD Pocket Dictionary:

TRANSITION – Passage from one state of action or subject to another.

TRANSITORY – of a passing nature, not long-lasting, merely temporary.

OUR little lives follow transition from birth through life to death. This WhatsApp group may wish to reflect upon Taxes at a later date.

Proust's Madeleine enabled him to recall the past, and we have all known an instant when scent or taste suddenly remind us of school, home, or an event in childhood.

Such jolts of recall occur quite unexpectedly. The olfactory bulb is part of the brain's limbic system and is closely associated with memory. Phillipe Jullian's illustrations for *Remembrance of Things Pas* are reproduced from his original etchings, and published by Chatto in 1970. The art editor designed these covers in black, blue, white and yellow, in topographic layout typical of its time.

Jullian's linear images are indistinctly printed black over a yellow ground. However, I have always though these images to be beautifully suited to the text.Jullian also illustrated Balzac, Dostoevsky, Wilde & Fairbank, which indicates his fascination with decadence, the macabre and an aesthetic life. Violet Trefusis was a friend, and Jullian's later years became tragic to a degree. After the death of his manservant, he hanged himself.

For a true understanding it has been said that one should read Proust in its original language. Alain-Fournier, Proust & Powell explore life's journey, sets of states, circumstances, actions, and the transitory nature of human existence. I have connected the pictorial art of their illustrators, who interpret the written word into appropriate designs, all for the purposes of publishing.

Below left is Marc's drawing of Charles Stringham for the first volume. As art students we were encouraged to appreciate 'negative space', of the intervals between things. This is a virtuoso demonstration of this approach.

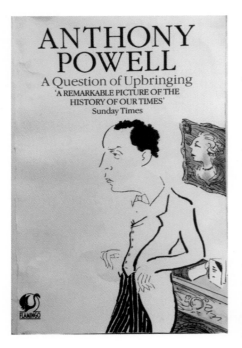

Within a restricted format, there is ample room for typography. Logotypes, and for our imagination to understand Stringham's appearance and character.

How to illustrate such formidable literature is difficult to fathom, to analyse. In terms of translation, another French novel. *Le Grand Meulnes* is as controversial as that of Proust's masterpiece.

Called *The Lost Estate* or *The Lost Domain*, such changes of title affect our perception. I chose it for our book group. No one liked it or enjoyed it. There was criticism of the translation, and of the plot, or lack of plot. either by Frank Davidson or Robin Buss. Much is lost in translation, of course.

However, I remain in great admiration for this book although reading it in English. The cover has been illustrated by Stanley Donwood, a fine contemporary artist who works with Radiohead and Robert Macfarlane. My copy has Alfred Sisley's *Small Meadows in Spring.* A painting which hangs in the Tate.

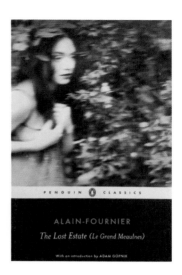

Another imprint has a photograph by Jeni Thompson. There is a girl running through shrubbery, bosom clasped. Each of these alters the character of the book, even before one has begun to read it.

Back to Transition.

Life's journey, its passage, has been likened to a river. In song, poetry and literature.

Such metaphors or symbols are familiar. The road, the highway, and so on. One can sell one's soul to the Devil at the crossroads. These flowing places represent the passage of time and transience of life. Mark Boxers's cover-art for Anthony Powell's *Dance to the Music of Time* depicts the dramatis personae of this twelve volume set of novels. Each drawing is understated, economical almost a cartoon, but most cleverly observed. Marc, as he was known, drew for newspapers and was married to Anna Ford. Powell's text covers a wide scope of history. Its people and places interweave through time and events. It is fiction, but based upon reality. From whom is Widmerpool derived, for example?

These are English novels, written in that language. There have been adaptions to TV, theatre, and film. Does the authenticity of Powell's text survive such transition?

RM: Book covers are so important and influential in the success of the text in between. Interesting you mention Violet Trefussis, an Edmonstone from Duntreath. In my memoir of Brodrick Haldane (cover designed by Descript – sadly no individual named) he writes about visiting her in Florence. He suggests she was rather spoiled.

RM: Mark Boxer was a genius who died far too soon. Poor old rather ghastly Widmerpool. I think I read somewhere that he was based on Powell's brother-in-law Lord Longford and the Lord Chancellor Reginald Manningham Buller. One of the greatest fictional characters of all time.

MLM: Jonny loved your observations and illustration of those ...great as always.

AB Jonny I too love the grand meaulnes your piece is wide reaching and fascinating. By the way Harold Wilson was the inspiration for Widerpool and at dinner at Balmoral, Camilla talked very fondly of her aunt Violet who was a great influence on her early life

JG: I think that Edward Heath is sometimes mentioned, too. In my youth, my mother gave me *Portrait of a Marriage* to read, for some reason. This was exciting stuff,

AB: I saw an interview in which he said all his characters were composites but he admitted Widerpool was mainly modelled on Wilson and yes, Nicholson's portrait is extraordinarily frank for a stiff upper lip English diplomat

Correction. Nigel Nicholson was never a diplomat. Like his father Harold he was a Conservative MP.

JG: Nigel Nicholson's account of his parents' relationship, in which Violet Trefusis plays a significant part. This was racy stuff, and most impressively grand and passionate. At about the same time, my parents took various newspapers and magazines, and I got to know Mark Boxer's drawings from the *Observer* and *New Statesman.* By that time I knew that I wanted to be an artist, and certainly did not consider these kinds of things to be art. Likewise Gerard Hoffnung's drawings. These are light, humorous, cartoonish etc. The skill is well hidden, as with Marc, effortlessly stylish. My outlook has become more broad-minded in terms of what can be art and what is meant by the word 'design'. Such categories are not always helpful in the 21st century, open for discussion. However, they do come into play when one has to consider employment as an artist. Art College is wonderful, all of it, and I absolutely loved it. It is after graduation that the question of employment arises, how to earn something for one's work.

CMS: Yes – fascinating. Do you judge a book by its cover or a cover by the book?

(handwritten margin note top: "why 2 colums?")

Dorothy Jackson

I taught for 38 years in the same school. I went from rookie teacher to one of the old ones!

(handwritten: "John")

When I started teaching I was qualified to teach Accounting, Secretarial Studies and my favourite, Economics. Along the way, Computing was added to the mix. When I read Roddy's piece about typewriters it brought back the memory of of sitting in a room of 20 pupils, with 20 manual typewriters hammering away.

Another teacher, from a different department, entered my room one day and wondered how I could stand the noise!

The class were silent, getting on with their work. She was referring to the noise of the typewriters. I was quite oblivious to the noise.

The typewriters were already 'ancient' when I started in 1977. Indeed, I spent much of my time fixing them. One day a pupil raised her hand and announced that 'her typewriter had run out of words!'

The ribbon had stuck and as I was fixing it, I mentioned that that part of the typewriter should have been automatic. She looked at me and said,' It's not automatic – it's awa tae hell!'

When I recounted the story in the Staff Room, one of the English teachers said he could imagine me in the morning filling the typewrite up with words.

(handwritten: "typewriter", "space", "pace?")

Another Department Head I had was keen to hold on to the typewriters even after we were starting to get computers. As the typewriters gradually broke, she touted around other schools for replacements. This unfuriated our Advisor who sent a note to all departments in the division asking if any of them had typewriters they didn't need and, if so, to get them ready for uplift to Lanark Grammar – or Romania!

(handwritten: "infuriated")

We were really amused by this. Not so my Head of Department.

The first computers we had were BBC's and also Apple Macintosh. What a relief when we got them.

Mind you, they were not networked and didn't have Internet. Again, I spent much of my time with a screw driver or a pair of tweezers. Finally, we moved over to a managed service on PCs. I missed the Apple Mac's though. Much more intuitive, I thought.

When it came to skills taught in schools by 1977, not many taught shorthand. I had not been taught shorthand at school but a friend's wife taught me at night. It was Pitman's Shorthand, and it is one of the most fascinating things I have ever learned.

I struggled with my speed as I had not been immersed in it at school. I used to sit in church and try and imagine the sermons in shorthand. Not such a bad thing as I was usually not much interested in the sermon.

I was 21 years old when I started teaching and had a S6 Tutor Group. That felt quite strange to me as I was not much older than some of the class! They were very respectful and I found them to be pleasant as they did not take advantage of me. I felt in control but different from them.

Living in a small community, I still bump into some of them in Lanark and I'm usually greeted with the phrase, 'Hello Miss.'

Teachers, after marriage, still retain the title 'Miss.' Andrew still struggles to call my colleague and friend by his given name rather than 'Sir' – even though Andrew attended his wedding and was a regular for dinner at our house. It doesn't seem to matter what age you are.

Whilst out walking, I regularly bump into an old teacher I had at school and adopt the strategy of not calling him anything.

I suppose one of the major transitions that anyone goes through is from the world of work to retirement. Some people don't have such a distinct line, but for me it was the right decision. I would not have been able to enjoy the relaxation that retirement offered me if the thought of still working part-time was lurking in the background. I did not particularly enjoy job-sharing for that reason. I had a wonderful job-sharer and long-time friend, but still felt my whole week was dominated by teaching.

I'm not very good with transitions; I don't like change. Maybe, because I've been lucky, my life has improved in many ways. but I'm also aware of all the sadness and unrest in the world. My parents worked to give me a better life than they had and, on one level, it was a success. Now I'm wondering about all the changes that are happening and trying not to be selfish.

CS: Great Dorothy - quite a difference in teaching styles from when you started to when you retired, I imagine.

RM: Good read Dorothy. One of the good things about those large manual typewriters is that they taught me to type and prepared me for the keyboards when the word processors arrived. However, can't say such progress has necessarily made life easier - have just been struggling to remember one of my dozen or more passwords!!

DJ: One of the best things I ever did was become a touch typist! Another was learning to ski. Can I ask you if you know Graeme Stewart a Silversmith from Dunblane. I think he mentioned he knew you. I think his business maybe closed and wondered if you knew anything. He was very nice and his work was superb. Dorothy x

MLM: Roddy loved your piece and as I'm reading Julian Barnes book *Man in The Red Coat*. The characters you introduced initially have also become 'friends'. Admire what your doing with the photos.

Pat Watson

NORMAN Buchan (MP Renfrewshire, West) was reported in Hansard as stating:
"In 1979 there were 106,000 unemployed in Strathclyde. Today there are over 200,000… almost all of those people have been unemployed for over 6 months. There is a static army of unemployed with the despair and hopelessness that that entails… The Government have failed to fulfil their promises and have even failed with the economic measures that they believe in. Their policies have been motivated by dogma and by an irrational hostility to the public sector.

Comparing the unemployment in Paisley, Renfrewshire with the job availability, there is only one job for every 32 people unemployed. The town of Johnstone, which includes Linwood in its employment area, has only one job vacant for every 114 people unemployed.

How have the Government responded? Their first response is that there is no alternative which is a declaration of the Government's impotence. Secondly, they have attacked the very sections of the community that suffer most. Despite the situation, there has been a 5 per cent cut in unemployment benefit. The Government have removed from the unemployed their earnings-related supplement and there has been a 5 per cent abatement. A married man receiving £40.45 is losing £13 a week because of the Government cuts in benefit. He should be receiving £13 a week more. He has lost one third of the income that he would have received under the old form of benefits. A married man with two children loses a total of £17 per week as a result of Government cuts.

In the Government's apparent dislike of the unemployment that they have created, they have made the unemployed pay the penalty."

These words sadly are as relevant today. I remember well the abject misery experienced by many people who could not find a job in the early 1980's including me for a time. Reflecting on the likely severity of unemployment due to the mishandling of the current appalling plague I remembered attending a hospitality event for marchers in 1983 at Barrhead and won't be surprised to see more People's March's for Jobs in 2021. Dick Gaughan performed at the Barrhead event. I was irritated though to be sitting near a group of teenagers who chatted loudly and animatedly throughout the whole performance. Turned out to be Gaughan's daughter and friends.

He sang from *Handful of Earth* including Ed Pickford's *Workers Song*.

We're the first ones to starve
We're the first ones to die.
We're the first in line
For that pie-in-the-sky…
But we're always the last
When the cream is shared out
For the worker is working
When the fat cat's about…
And always expected
To carry the can.

Sadly not much has changed over the passage of time from 1982/3 to 2020. I feel for the many people whose lives will be so cruelly disrupted, dreams and hope for the future consigned to be no more than a past memory.

In *The Guardian* of June 16th 2020: Tony Wilson, the Institute for Employment Studies' director, said:

"If the public health crisis is just starting to ease, today's figures show that the unemployment crisis is only just beginning.

There can be no doubt now that we are on course for claimant unemployment of 3 million by next month, and it may well reach the highest ever recorded."

Our Governments never appear to learn from past mistakes or reflect. It also manifestly failed to swiftly lockdown to protect our population and businesses.

NEW HORIZONS

Dorothy Jackson

THIS is an interesting topic during this pandemic as there has been plenty of time to contemplate potential new horizons or, in my case, renewing horizons. I've decided to reminisce about a place that until 1966 was a small Scottish village, Aviemore.

I first holidayed in Aviemore in 1968 with my family. I was excited about going there as I had heard much about 'The Centre', the creation of Sir Hugh Fraser of Allander and the architect John Poulson. This was to be a new kind of tourist attraction.

The Aviemore Centre was built on the site of the Aviemore Hotel and its golf courses, which was destroyed by fire in 1950. It was opened by Lady Fraser of Allander (wife of Sir Hugh who owned House of Fraser) in 1966. The centre, as it became known, quickly developed into a major Scottish tourist destination as it had an ice rink which was used for skating and curling, a cinema, a swimming pool, function rooms big enough to host the Hunt Ball and conferences and many hotels and self-catering choices for accommodation. There was even a dry ski slope, go-karting and Santa Clause Land (which was open all year!). In 1968, when I first visited it, I stayed with my parents in their touring caravan!

The Centre was a special place, very modern by the standards then. Some say that the original intention was to have a roof over the centre but that was never done.

I returned to Aviemore both as a teacher and tourist many times after that. I learned to ski there and from 1980 until about 1989, I spent many weekend both with friends and with school groups. It was then the perfect place to holiday in the UK in the winter. Even if the snow was not good, the village offered other attractions.

Learning to ski opened up new horizons for me. I no longer waited for the Summer to go on holiday, but saved furiously to have a winter holiday too. I got a job with a minor player in the ski holiday industry and some years I was able to have 3 ski holidays and many weekends on a teacher's budget. I made many new friends who have become life long ones. Skiing is the kind of sport that incorporates skill and a lot of socialising. If it had not been for Aviemore and its infrastructure, I doubt that I would have been able to pursue it.

Aviemore is in the heart of the Cairngorms and is there to serve the skiers, cyclists, walkers and mountaineers who flock there. It is a year round resort. The Centre survived good and bad snow years but by 1998 was looking rundown and in need of a huge injection of funds. Many of The Centre buildings were demolished. It was given a £50million overhaul replacing many of the accommodation buildings but not many of the leisure buildings. By 2006, when we got our house in Aviemore, there was a group of locals trying to make Aviemore a popular tourist destination again.

Our house in Aviemore was going to offer us a new dimension on our life. We had been in Aviemore at Easter 2006 and my aunt was keen to buy one of the new houses that were being built in the village. We signed for the house at the beginning of May and she died five days later. We went ahead with the purchase and got the house at the end of June 2006.

I often wonder what was going on in her mind at that time. She was a determined woman who at the age of 81 had never ever seen a doctor. She must have known she was unwell but managed to see the house and was determined to get it.

I'm writing this whilst in Aviemore, having returned after almost 16 weeks of lockdown. It looks to me that there will be changes due to businesses closing and others opening up.

I hope the Village survives as a tourist attraction. It's beginning to come alive again after the lockdown and there are some visitors enjoying the scenery.

PW: A lovely contribution Dorothy and great photos. My son mentioned being up that way last week. Aviemore was surprisingly quiet but Loch Morlich busy! Strange times indeed. Very lovely part of the world. X

MM: Wow what scenery Dorothy. Your connection to it through the recounting of the town's and your own history comes across as clear and refreshingly as the water in that loch! I want to come up and dive in too.

MS: Great piece Dorothy. Brought back memories of going up to Aviemore as a child. I thought it was the most modern exciting place to go especially the penny arcades and the ice rink. Learnt to ski there too.

Marie-Louise Brulatour Mills

Boston Touchdown

TWO signatures are scribbled on documents today, one of a promissory note and the second, a rental contract for 260 Beacon Street. Both ear mark a fresh start in a turn-of-the-century apartment overlooking the Charles River and my husband's entrance into Harvard Business School, after a year in Viet Nam. It is promising.

The transition resembled the colour changes (I hope in the autumn leaves outside), from a lush green to a striking red. I look out the French door that leads to a small balcony overlooking the Charles River with a selection of single and eight men skulls rowing down its calm waters. Years of moving homes to exchange his Naval Academy education in Phantom jets is now over after a year of his dropping Napalms on America's adversaries. Since his return from Nam his total lack of interest in the family becomes poignant and the grounds for a separation.

I whip up souffles, cook Beef Bourguignon or curries of various flavour but all my efforts in the kitchen go unnoticed. He sleeps off a hangover while I had to drive myself to hospital after my waters broke to have my second child an hour later.

He hacks down all my sunflowers in our garden in our last home and all that becomes too much. The last straw prompts my suggestion of a separation.

"Yes and I want meat and potatoes and not fancy French food," he tells me during that discussion a month before this move but we concur to try again to repair a damaged marriage. We settle in, but within the first month he packs his bag and leaves. He pays back my loan and, at the same time, finds another woman.

Days with two children are rich with a sliding scale of happiness to sadness. Harpsichord concerts at home enrich my days. My daughter's first birthday is spent on a blanket by the Charles River.

After the exchange of presents, I try to cut into the especially made ice cream birthday cake. The wax paper separating her favourite ice cream flavours is left in and we three melt with laughter just as the raspberry sherbet that drips down Yvonne's pale cheeks on her smocked dress with a rose bud design.

Not all days spell laughter. My first date rings the bell, my son screams and yells. I don't recall if I left the apartment. Only my job of Fashion Director at Bonwit Teller drags me out daily.

My husband marries and has another two more children, and since my move to Italy thirty years ago he never attempts to see our children. At twenty years old, my son calls him and there begins a relationship.

For him this is a new horizon.

RM: Very poignant Marie- Louise...

PW: Oh Marie Louise, so very moving. X

Beautifully written as well

BD: Marie-Louise, very pictorial recall of that time in your life. The sunflowers were symbolic, surely. Many thanks. Barbara.

DJ: I know Boston quite well and your description of it is both colourful and sad. I visit my friend in Concord MA every year and I'm missing it this year. X

Callum Stark

NEW Horizons is one of those clichés par excellence that seems to forever ring of sickly sunsets and the brimming optimism of those we don't like. But it's far more complex than all that. This one's really bowled me for six as evidenced by the number of scrawling false starts for this piece in my notebook (exhibits below).

Horizons are only ever perfect when they are just that, horizons – glowing attractively in the distance. It's so easy, natural, tempting and occasionally delicious to think of that to come as a silver bullet: remedy to any and all present unhappiness.

But when we do reach that halcyon land of our imaginings it's rarely so two-dimensional as to be perfect. Instead, that new horizon will have much in common with that which we thought had been left behind. No matter the context, it too will be a composite of good and bad.

I'm keenly aware of this as I prepare to leave home this autumn, hopefully for Cambridge, maybe for Glasgow. I know it won't be perfection but it will be new, and that's sounding pretty close to perfection right now.

CS: This is perhaps my most pitiful entry to Decameron, and pales in comparison to the brilliance demonstrated in the last ten days. I'm sorry not to end our 100 days on a more resounding, satisfying and neat note, as done so skilfully by all of you but here it is. Where normally the pressure of the eleventh hour is my comfort zone, today I have found it merely stressful. If something profound comes to me lying on a hillside in a week or so's time, I'll write. Here's this for now. See you in 5.

PW: 'St Kilda Cragsmen' acrylic on paper, North Rona in the alcove. Photo DJCAD tribute exhibition.

PW: Wishing you the very best of luck with your plans for your future Callum and thank you for your considerable patience.

Roddy Martine

THERE is a poem often employed at funerals. It concerns a ship, an object of great beauty and strength sailing into the morning breeze, and just where the sea meets the sky, someone says "There, she is gone!"

Out of sight. But gone where?

And just at that moment, on another shore, there are other eyes and other voices and a cry goes up, "Here she comes!"

Regardless of metaphors, the crossing of any horizon is a voyage of faith into the unknown. How often have any of us imagined or hankered after pastures new? That is until we find ourselves there, of course.

Sorting through some old photographs I recently came across a bundle of negatives from my first sojourn into North America. It was 1977.

As a magazine editor and Scot, I had been invited to the Grandfather Mountain Highland Games in North Carolina and a chance meeting with the General Manager of British Airways in Glasgow had led him to offer me a free flight on Concorde. You can imagine my excitement. Concorde, the sleek swallow of the skies had by then existed for less than nine years. To this day, I have recall of watching its maiden ascent into Edinburgh from the windows of my parents' home on Corstorphine Hill.

America entranced me. I loved the "idea" of America. Childhood memories are of those mesmerising black and white Fred Astaire and Ginger Rogers musicals followed by a stream of technicolour – *Oklahoma, West Side Story,* and *Seven Brides for Seven Brothers.* My USA was that of Mark Twain, Tennessee Williams, Scott Fitzgerald, Dorothy Parker, Betty MacDonald, Jack Kerouac, Margaret Mitchell and Saul Bellow, whom I'd recently encountered in the bar of Edinburgh's Cafe Royal.

America was my new horizon.

So it was off to the States from Heathrow in style, landing four hours later on the 4th July in Washington. Contrary to expectation the flight itself, apart from witnessing the curve of the earth through a haze of alcohol, was not particularly memorable. The cabin space was cramped. I drank four gin and tonics in the VIP lounge before take-off, drank a bottle of Merlot and two mini bottles of Port in transit, and signed up for the Mile High Club which was not at all what I thought it might be.

The big excitement, of course, was that I was going to America.

I was met at Dulles Airport by Donald "Doughnut" Campbell, Sennachie of Clan Campbell USA, who whisked me off to a pool party in Arlington, every Scottish boy's rights of passage wet dream of what America ought to be like – champagne cocktails and peach ice cream, bronze muscle toned blue eyed boys and girls with sparkling white teeth and bathing trunks, bikinis and thongs to die for.

I purchased a white silk suit in the nearest Mall and took the midnight train to Georgia. Safely ensconced in my roomette, I innocently asked the huge African American attendant to knock me up when we reached Clemson in South Carolina. I never saw him again.

But on the Clemson platform in the mist of an early dawn was my friend Peter Wilson from Ayrshire, a student at Clemson University, who had volunteered to drive me north to Sugar Mountain In North Carolina. There we were scheduled to meet up with Andrew MacThomas of Finegand, clan chief of one of Scotland's smallest clans (Thomson, Thomas, Thom, MacCombie) but big enough to be escorted the previous weekend by the film star Elizabeth Taylor and her then US Senator husband John Warner at the Virginia Highland Games.

The largest of over one hundred or more Scottish gatherings throughout the continent, Grandfather Mountain Highland Games was in its 21st year. Peter, Andrew and I were still in our twenties, desperate to embrace everything we touched and while to some extent dumbstruck by the tartan-clad absurdity that surrounded us, we were easily won over by the sheer exotic nonsense, colour, fun, kindness and vibrancy of it all.

From all across America they came, sixty thousand or more ex-patriate Scots, all of them intent on celebrating their ancestral Scottish roots and origins, swarming annually to spend the weekend under the breath of a hot sun consuming the lush pastureland of MacRae's Meadows and thickly wooded slopes of Grandfather.

There were caravans and tents and trailers and every motel in the neighbourhood was booked solid. Over its history, immigrant Scots have done rather well in America. It might appear rather tragic, even comical to those of us living in the mother country but this is the uncompromising way they like to make whoopee.

In the evenings, the hillsides resembled a vast stage set for the television series *Outlander*, or Mel Gibson's film *Braveheart*. During the day, there was caber tossing, putting the shot, kilted wrestling, tugs-o-war, trials of strength, parades, piping and Highland dancing. I met the singing Macdonald Gammon family, direct descendants of Flora herself. I took part in a Clan Cameron march.

At a dinner on the Saturday night, my "date" was the steel tycoon Andrew Carnegie's grand-daughter. Bunny Miller. The difference in our ages was irrelevant. We had a ball.

At a barbecue on the last night I met Stephanie who invited me to inspect her condominium in Atlanta which, as it transpired, was a pool-side bungalow in a district called, familiarly enough, Morningside.

The Spanish Moss, mint tulips, palladian mansions and magnolias of the Deep South worked their magic. I was in love. I could live here. I would marry Scarlet O'Hara. I'd never be hungry again!

For the following fortnight I basked in the steamy sunshine and lived the American dream, taking passage on a Savannah Riverboat, admiring the nowadays considered politically incorrect Confederate carvings on Stone Mountain, dancing all night in open air restaurants under the stars.

But then reality struck. Or was it culture shock?

Stephanie kept a handgun in the top drawer of her bedside table. Not that this bothered me over much but It definitely disconcerted me when we were turned away by armed guards from the famous Peach Tree Plaza because I was wearing blue jeans. When I challenged them, I was told there was a dress code. I, and the "blacks from the car park", were not welcome.

"We don't have problems like that in the UK," I said snootily. "Oh yes, you do," came the response. "Birmingham."

At a travelling art exhibition, I commented upon Picasso's pink period. Stephanie thought this hilarious. "I suppose you'd call that one over there his blue period?" she squealed. I realised it would never work.

The fortnight came to an end and I escaped into a Big Apple slowly recovering from an electric storm. As the yellow cab catapulted me downtown, I noted the vandalised shop fronts and warehouses. A friend working for Reuter's put me up on his sofa and the following day showed me the Frick and the roof of the World Trade Centre. I took the ferry to Staten Island and appraised the usual tourist sights. There was a job on offer.

But by then the novelty had worn off. I wanted to go home. I have since returned to the United States many times for a variety of reasons and along the way acquired many dearly loved American friends. But do I ever regret not taking that job in New York?

The answer is a resounding no. When I consider what has since taken place in the world's largest democracy, I thank God I decided to stay where I am. Besides, such horizons are no longer new to me, no matter how big and powerful, glamorous or intoxicating they might seem.

But when the time comes – not yet I hasten to add – I do still rather like the idea of a ship and an out-of- sight shore, and a chorus crying out, "Here he comes!"

BD: Thanks Roddy. So funny and entertaining. Andrew Carnegie's daughter? Most impressed as a Dunfermline girl!

RM: Bunny Miller. A great lady. xx

PW: What a grand experience Roddy. One of my daughter's took herself to US at a similar age but her experience the opposite of yours. Moira was interested in Mike Kelley's work and wanted to experience Detroit for herself. She now lives in Michigan.

CMS: Fantastic Roddy! I was at the Grandfather Mountain Games with my Dad in 1981 who was president of the Stuart Society and guest of honour. It was hilarious- the Americans took their Scottishness so seriously and will never forget the Stars and Stripes tartan!

RM: I've actually been to it twice Catherine - I was there in 1980 with Scotworld, a travel company I set up with the MacThomas - all very surreal but I had great fun. I think I remember your Dad telling me he had been.

Andrew Brown

I am writing this last contribution to our modern Decameron with mixed emotions on a train from Edinburgh to London in a carriage meant for 72 passengers but contains only half-a-dozen masked travellers suitably distanced from each other.

I left Scotland in the late afternoon and the evening light as the sun sets on the horizon is illuminating the clouds from below like a Turner painting which cannot but uplift my spirits despite doubts about what is to come over the next few months.

I have not hated this lockdown as much as I thought I would; indeed it has given me breathing space and the opportunity to look into myself and concentrate on the value of family and friends and how precious our personal connections and interactions are.

It has enabled me to spring clean the entire cottage even tidying out the cupboard under the stairs until there was no displacement activity left to prevent me from painting. Of course, I have enormously enjoyed and will miss our communal intercourse over this literary and artistic endeavour of ours. It's difficult to believe that a hundred days have passed since we began at the beginning of the lockdown so although I have trepidations I am full of hope for the future too, looking forward to writing and painting more and spending quality time with those I love.

Mark Muller Stuart – New Horizons

FIRST of all, I loved Andrew's piece – including its brevity and succinctness. That is something which by now you will all realise I'm not capable of. It's the barrister in me, so I apologise for the length of this piece. Once again, I have divided it into two parts.

Part One contains some personal reflections on lockdown. Part Two focuses on new horizons and some of the choices likely to confront Scotland. Don't feel obliged to read both!

Part One: Some Personal Reflections.

Like Andrew I'm not quite sure about what's to come. People talk about – and almost lazily assume – that we must and will be returning to what many characterise or describe as a 'new normal'. I don't sense that at all. I think the pandemic will change our perspectives about everything – from how we personally live our lives to how we organise ourselves socially and politically onto what things society will value.

Lockdown, I now realise, has risen like a phoenix or New Horizon to cast new lights and shadows across our universe. It has become both a looking-glass and mirror through which to question and examine our settled existence. It certainly literally stopped me in my physical tracks as I travelled around the world on behalf of the United Nations and the London School of Economics. In an instant I was sent home by the UN despite the pandemic putting into perspective how futile and dangerous violent conflict is for our inter-dependent globalised world.

But it would be disingenuous for me if I did not admit how I have almost treasured the space and time that lockdown has given me personally. I have been given time to get fit, lose weight, buy an electric bike and tour hitherto unexplored parts of the Scottish Borders. I have been given space to think through and devise a new course for the LSE on conflict resolution and political transition, which I will now teach in the lent term of 2021.

I have been given the opportunity to write an important paper I have wanted to write on the catastrophic legal and humanitarian failure of the international system to help civilian populations in conflict-affected areas where non-state actors control large swathes of territory but the international community does nothing for fear of attacking the sovereignty of host states who are either unwilling or unable to protect their own citizens in those areas.

And I have been given the joy of encountering and enjoying the perspective and histories of friends, old and new, as a consequence of Andrew's inspired decision to create Decameron. It is a testament to him and the confidence he inspires in all of us that we have all given and felt able to share something of ourselves during these testing times.

But above all lockdown has enable me to spend more time with Catherine and my family at Traquair. When I joined the UN five years ago, I knew I would spend a considerable time away. But nothing prepared me for just how much, as the Syrian and Yemen conflicts deepened. As I caught six flights a week for the next few years, Isabella and Louis did their exams and moved away to University, while Charlotte edged closer to doing so. Then lockdown happened and we all came back to stay at Traquair. It was as if the Gods had given me back time itself.

Over the next four months, we dined, swam in the Tweed, played rounders, tennis and charades together. Catherine and I met their girlfriends and boyfriends, helped them deal with splitting up from some of them, and talked about their and our futures. Our children helped paint rooms, transcribe papers in our private archives, pack beer to keep some money coming in and made short video tours about the history of the house for our Trust. I bought Charlotte a lovely red striped Mini for her birthday.

In the meantime, Catherine managed to get Dolores, our young King Charles Spaniel, impregnated by a dog from Jedburgh – despite the travails of social distancing – only for us to discover two weeks later that our other fifteen year old King Charles Spaniel, Delilah, is likely to slip away sometime soon due to impending kidney failure. New horizons indeed.

But I for one will be eternally grateful for being given the unexpected chance to experience these quiet magical family moments of happiness and sadness. Moments which sometimes included Andrew, who along with Delilah, helped usher in Charlotte's 18th birthday last Wednesday, by playing rounders with her friends in the reddest felt trousers and snakeskin winkle-pickers I have ever seen, complete with Michael in a dog's collar.

Yet, I am also acutely conscious of how easy it is for Catherine and I to enjoy lockdown living at Traquair with its open hills, glistening waters and private tennis court in the back. What I have just recounted is almost distasteful set against the experiences of other people. Each week we watched with increasing horror how the pandemic destroyed the health of people and ripped communities apart.

It is without doubt a viscous and capricious beast that I sometimes think was sent to test us our resolve – to give us one last chance to demonstrate that the arc of history does indeed bend towards justice, as Martin Luther King once said it does. For if lockdown has revealed anything, it is not just the shoddy, second-rate nature of our present governance systems, but the endemic economic and social inequalities that predominate within our society – inequalities that have always bubbled just below the surface, but which we as a society have conveniently failed to empathise with or see.

I strongly believe that any new horizons that appear after lockdown will have to confront these ills if we are to have any chance of escaping further conflict and division. Yet I am not without hope. With crisis comes new perspectives and resolve. Necessity, they say, is the mother of invention. Humans can adapt and usher in sudden change quickly if so required. I witnessed the capacity of indentured human beings to rise up against their oppressors in 1989 in Prague, in 2014 in Kiev, and in 2011 across the Arab World, which is once again on the move.

The push for greater equality and freedoms, as well as for responsive government, although not always successful, is on the march again. I believe such visions and horizons can prevail but only with human solidarity and inspired leadership. What many have discovered during lockdown, including us through Decameron, is a renewed sense and commitment to human and social solidarity. There is a growing belief that we are ultimately stronger for focusing on what unites rather than divides us. It is why I believe Trump will fail to be elected in November as the possibility of a new beginning and set of new horizons galvanises a bruised, but in some senses, becalmed world.

Part Two: Reflections on Scotland's Future.

WHICH leads me to back to Scotland. As I think I have eluded to in an earlier Decameron, during lockdown I have been researching a book on Cyrus Griffin, the last President of the Continental Congress of the thirteen states of America, who eloped with Christina Stuart, the eldest daughter of the 6th Earl of Traquair in the early 1770s.

I have had the unique privilege to be able to leaf through the Traquair archives and library to discover new facts about their lives and times. A shiver has travelled down my back as I have read draft notes of letters later written by and to these characters – and come across pencilled in comments made by them in 18th Century pamphlets now bound in books in the library about the conflict between the Colonies and the British Empire. They speak of another era of turmoil where individuals had to make fundamental and quick decisions about where their loyalties lay both personally and politically.

As I have undertaken this research, I have been struck by how much has changed but also by how much of what they experienced remains relevant to our own existence today. When Cyrus arrived in Edinburgh in 1766 the Enlightenment was in full swing. New ideas about liberty and the backward tendencies of monarchical and religious domination swirled through the new literary salons.

By the time he left with his new wife for the New World the grasping and oppressive tentacles of British Empire had begun to reveal themselves. Within a few short years the American populous were in revolt as a pandemic of liberty swept across the water from their continent towards France.

The time it took for these new horizons of liberty to emerge within the consciousness of ordinary people was breathtakingly short. That such liberties were not extended to slaves, native Americans or women, has come back to haunt both America and its Founding Fathers, as the Black Lives Matter movement, which exploded during lockdown, attests.

Yet, despite these grave failings, the torch of liberty and right to self-determination was lit across the world, ultimately leading to the end of slavery, de-colonisation, the Me-Too movement and, of course, the return of devolved government to Scotland.

This point should not be lost on us as we emerge from lockdown and go to the polls next year to decide the direction Scotland should take. The American Revolution continues to grip the imagination today because although unique in some respects, it contains within it all the lessons a society needs to think about and heed when it comes to the business of self-determination and in ensuring a successful political and social transition.

A number of new horizons will be offered to us next year in circumstances where we will not be able to opt for the status quo of six years ago. We will be asked whether we want to either align ourselves to a Brexit universe where decisions about a new internal UK market will be increasingly taken by a UK government that Scotland did not vote for – an internal market that will be to the detriment of the current devolved arrangement, which was predicated on EU competencies prevailing in Scotland regarding the environment and the free movement of workers, goods and services.

Or whether we want to strike out on our own into a brave new world without the safety net of the Bank of England, the UK treasury, and the solidarity of the four nations. It is a monumental question for our country, which is why the American Revolution speaks to us.

Consider for a moment the opening words of the Declaration of Independence:

'When in the Course of human Events, it becomes necessary for one People to dissolve the Political Bonds which have connected them with another, and to assume among the Powers of the Earth, the separate and equal Station to which the Laws of Nature and of Nature's God entitle them, a decent Respect to the Opinions of Mankind requires that they should declare the causes which impel them to the Separation.

'We hold these Truths to be self-evident, that all Men are created equal, that they are endowed by their Creator with certain inalienable Rights, that among these are Life, Liberty, and the Pursuit of Happiness——That to secure these Rights, Governments are instituted among Men, deriving their just Powers from the Consent of the Governed, that whenever any Form of Government becomes destructive of these Ends, it is the Right of the People to alter or to abolish it, and to institute new Government, laying its Foundation on such Principles, and organising its Powers in such Form, as to them shall seem most likely to effect their Safety and Happiness.

'Prudence, indeed, will dictate that Governments long established should not be changed for light and transient Causes; and accordingly all Experience hath shewn, that Mankind are more disposed to suffer, while Evils are sufferable, than to right themselves by abolishing the Forms to which they are accustomed. But when a long Train of Abuses and Usurpations, pursuing invariably the same Object, evinces a Design to reduce them under absolute Despotism, it is their Right, it is their Duty, to throw off such Government, and to provide new Guards for their future Security.....'

Are these not the questions that we will also be asked to consider?

In the end, the American people chose full independence but interestingly managed to quickly negotiate a peace with George III, the hardest of foes, who within a year of losing the Colonies spoke of his desire that the natural bonds of kinship and commerce should bring the two nations closer together.

Such a full offer of independence was not put to the people by Alex Salmond in 2014 – with his diluted promise of the continued existence of the pound and rule of the Bank of England without so much as a Scottish vote on its Board.

This time it will be, and we will be asked to decide in favour of new liberties or a renewal once again of economic insurance in exchange for power.

What is clear from the American experience is that in choosing to cut free from the most powerful Empire in the world and to become fully independent, the American people had to fashion a completely new governance, judicial and financial system and enter into bold detailed diplomatic negotiations. The dispute between Hamilton and Jefferson over the assumption of the national debt and the creation of a central bank was just a manifestation of the reality of the stark decision they took.

That stark choice now confronts Scotland today. In the end, Hamilton won the argument and America assumed the debt to become one of the most dynamic republics that history has ever witnessed, although, as the travails of politics would have it, Jefferson took the fruits of his rival's endeavours, ensured the continuation of slavery, and assumed the crown of the new republic for himself.

We now have to make a similar choice. Should we continue with our pretend parliament (which only spends rather than raises revenue) - in a new era of Brexit cut from our European heritage – or assume massive obligations and risks to try to forge a new independent political future with new associations with both the UK and the EU, with all the change that this will entail?

One matter is clear to me – the decisions we take will define us including who we claim to be for the next hundred years – just as the scrawls of our forefathers and sisters did in the pamphlets in the Traquair library that I found 250 years later during lockdown.

Some say we should say yes as fortune favours the brave. But surely that is not enough. The reason why the Americans forged a viable revolution based upon republican principles, while the French did not, was because of the character of its people, which had both the inclination and skills to run a limited and representative system of self-government, devoid of despotism, with a central bank dedicated to promotion of its own interests. Scotland has undoubtedly the expert capacities to do the same, but the real question is whether it is has the confidence and ability to bear the risk over the short and medium term.

Lockdown has given us the chance to reflect upon these capacities and see government in action as we begin to make this fundamental choice.

Whatever Scotland chooses, it will be a new horizon for us all. Some have likened it to a decision between a revolution of the heart and the head. I believe that is a false characterisation.

It will need to be both, whatever we decide. There will be no looking back. And that is yet another reason why I have treasured both lockdown and Decameron. It has given me the chance, time, space and vehicle to think about these issues before we set new horizons for both ourselves and the country. Lockdown has helped me understand in what direction I want to go in the next few years.

I hope it has done the same for you – but even if it hasn't, I hope it has at least given some respite from the never-ending immediacy of the modern world. So, with that final thought in mind, lets us say Bravo to Andrew tonight in our final virtual drinks gathering for having the presence of mind to recall and reconstitute Decameron for the present Age.

Pin-board of postcards and perspective drawing.

Jonathan Gibbs

NEW: Now first made, invented, introduced, known, fresh, further, different, changed. etc. Thanks to everyone for excellent, inspiring correspondence.

Erudite, historical, humorous, literary and life-enhancing in so many ways I look forward to meeting in actuality, to raise a glass or two for Decameron.

New horizons beckon to whatever lies ahead. From an aeroplane one can appreciate the curvature of the earth, to see the sun set from a high perspective, several thousand feet up in the sky.

But that horizon always eludes us, being that point at which the surface of the earth disappears from view. This is aptly illustrated by *Panorama & News at Ten* graphics, digital tour-de-forces of screen-design with twirling globes.

At full-moon we can see but half of the Big Cheese. Even though we can always take a space-ship ride to see the dark side, but then the front half will not be visible, if you see what I mean. When a child is asked to draw the full-moon, he or she will draw a circle – the vertical cross-section of a sphere.

The line does not exist in reality, it is just a way of depicting something – as Eduard Manet so tightly said,"There are no lines in nature, only areas of colour, one against the other."

However, the drawn line can be a wonderful thing, such a useful pictorial divide. On a wide beach behind the sea we can just about see some curvature.

That line where the sea & sky meet. There might be an island, distant shore, storm, battleship, or the Spanish Navy approaching.

We cannot see it yet as we scour the horizon for enemies or for hope of rescue. But it is empty, nothing then a speck appears, then & so on.

Silhouettes are vertical cross-sections: sphere becomes circle, pyramid to triangle; cube to square; egg to oval. In contemporary art, this again is aptly illustrated by D. Hirst's *Mother & Child,* a vertical slice.

The outline of a cow contains all of its internal organs, within its shape. Dreadful. Hans Bellmer was good at nearly horizontal cross-sections, contours as with a globe mentioned above, but with bodies. These erotic and neurotic depictions are sliced up. Art students are encouraged to analyse the body, the life figure, by drawing such contours – but without eroticism, usually, if possible, or even neurosis, moving towards an unerstanding of form..

Spirit Level

Those lines on the Panorama globe are just simplified longitude & latitude, a graphic representation of horizons, divisions of the globe. Paintings of the past show vistas, horizons, landscapes with nearness and the far distance.

The invention of air travel, a new thing in its time, altered our perception of time and space. For it is difficult to separate these two things.

One could travel towards that Venetian or Florentine horizon by boat, carriage, on foot, horseback, or ship. Hockney's LA landscapes and Kossof's Kentish Town express landscape or cityscape where the car, train and aeroplane allow us to travel quickly without awareness of the terrain travelled. Pablo Picasso & George Braque wanted to paint a chair, guitar, still-life, or billiard table seeing this thing from several viewpoints in one picture. Hence the fragmentation & abstraction of art that followed this endeavour.

Going back to seeing half of the moon, or a chair, or a face, for that matter, I am content to see it from one viewpoint, and to try and draw it as I see it in that way. I am told that my eye-level, my line of sight, gives me the position of the horizon. If I lie down on the beach, looking seawards, that horizon is lowered accordingly. I can use a plumb-line to get a true vertical, and my spirit level for the precise horizontal. My iPhone will do none of these things which is impressive, of course, but I also like to use antique or analogue tools for artistic pursuits, design & craftsmanship.

Plumb Line.

Jessie Ann Matthew

Dear everyone,

I hate goodbyes, but love hellos – so here is a final one.

Many thanks to Andrew for organising this project and all your amazing contributions. Andrew, Mark and Catherine, you have all summed up brilliantly the current situation. So mine this week is purely personal.

HORIZONS OLD

When lockdown started I was all set to continue my painting project which I had begun in the previous months.

I am working towards an exhibition at Glen, scheduled for September, now postponed. Suddenly at lockdown, we had two grown-up children + girlfriend in the house, for more than 100 days, lovely and life affirming in many ways.

Delicious meals, walks, swims in the river. Wonderful birdsong and glorious flowers as Spring turned into Summer. But I have to say that I have not enjoyed this period like some of you. I have found concentrating on work and keeping positive very hard. Which leads us to

HORIZONS – NEW.

Looking forward now to getting on with my project, putting brush to board and capturing the landscape in and around Peebles. So not goodbye but as they say, adieu and hopefully to raise a glass and jolly banter.

JM: Transition was Marks suggestion and we put forward New Horizons. Scheduled to be the last unless we all vote for an epilogue!

PW: Thanks Jessie. It helps. What was your idea New Horizons? Someone on the radio the other day, didn't catch who, suggested we need more pessimism in Scotland so we can feel better if things turn out better than awful!

PW: Didn't want to mislead their kids...

JM: The cup half full syndrome.

I wanted a topic that might take us forwards that could be interpreted by words or pictures.x

PW: Great, that helps a lot Jessie. The gag was from Andy Zaltman, Breaking the News.

PW: Remembering a good book exploring children's transexual by Jenni Fagan, The Sunlight Pilgrims.

Pat Watson

I think this has to be my contribution.

So many mixed, conflicting feelings. Found this painting this week from Alan's St Kilda series.

THANK you all, going to miss the shared experience.

Alan wrote to me from St Kilda. "This place is so wild and exposed the ever present wind clears my brain constantly, love sitting at the cliff edge and watching the fulmars fly past me sometimes only 2 feet away. They hardly beat their wings and just float with the up-currents of the cliff face.

I still think it's a sad place, watch this space for lots of spooky ghostly pictures, flying clergymen included."

And so he did.

MM: Pat what an extraordinary evocative image. Thank you for sharing. It's visceral and temporal and intimate and boundless - at least from my perspective.

CS: Pat, that first painting is such a beauty!

PW: It is possible many imagine living on extreme islands is a quiet life, but it was unbelievably noisy, nesting birds, seals, sea and wind. At least that was Alan's experience.

CMS: Beautiful images Pat - really capture St Kilda

ML: Spectacular painting so full of soul and strength x ml

BD: Goodbye Andrew and thank you for being so positive and proactive in this little departure from our ghastly and nightmare situation. Happy Landings and haste ye back!

ML: Andrew beautiful and both words and photos encapsulate all. Thank you my dear again for our long and colourful ridexxxx

Catherine Maxwell Stuart

WE will all have our own memories of this lock down period and there has been a unique chance to reflect on our lives that has been evident in the many brilliant contributions in our Decameron but looking forward is a much more challenging task.

As time passes, the way we think about this period will change so I thought I would briefly chronicle my memories of lockdown as we begin to emerge into a strange new world.

Phase 1: March/April.

THE first death from Corona virus in the UK is announced on March 5th. We are preparing to open the house to the public on 1st April. We have our annual staff meeting on 12th March and we are asked if we will be having to have hand sanitiser at the door and drop tickets into boxes. I say I hope it doesn't come to that.

We attend a tourism business networking event on the 16th March with over a 100 tourism businesses from the Scottish Borders. By this time the virus is a big topic of conversation but still no one is talking about closing their doors. The next day one of our staff reports she is asthmatic and no longer wants to work in the house for at least 12 weeks.

My office staff are getting edgy except for Lydia who is 22 and looks astonished that anything might happen to disturb her normal routine. We decide to delay opening until 1st May. The next day Nicola announces schools are to close that Friday. Poor Charlotte, who is 17 and in her final year suddenly sees the last of her school days disappear and exams cancelled. She begs us to allow her to go to the pub for the final time to see her friends. Mark and I swither and then allow her to go for an hour. Full lockdown is called on the 23rd March.

How quickly our lives are turned upside down. Suddenly, we all gather round the TV for the daily press conference which cannot be missed. It feels like wartime. I am the designated shopper and spend days fixated on finding a bag of rice or flour. From panic buying the atmosphere changes into a sombre realisation that this situation is going to last well into the future. We queue outside the supermarket and there is little conversation.

I spend the first couple of weeks of lockdown in the office fielding phone calls cancelling events, weddings, and b&b bookings. I start to frantically re-work budgets, ring the bank and talk to our staff. The furlough announcement is a godsend and then we hear we are eligible for some small business grants. We can safely go into hibernation for three months and then think about the future.

Then, Spring arrives in all its heavenly corona defying beauty. We take long walks, spend more time outside. I get fascinated by birdsong and download an app. One day I find myself sitting in a wood listening to birds when I look up I see a huge tawny owl staring down at me. The wildlife becomes tamer, undisturbed by people or cars. The deer become positively precocious getting nearer the house and finally I capture a photograph on one on the avenue.

Phase 2: May/June

A sense of resignation creeps in among all of us. This lockdown is going to last longer than we all expected. Will we be able to open the house at all this year? Is it worth opening the grounds? For the first time in my life we are living at Traquair House in the Spring and there is no one else around. This must have been what it was like a hundred years ago. Part of me is loving every minute and part is missing other people to share this experience.

We have the added bonus of having all our children back at home – they are brilliant. It is not easy for them. Their plans on hold, a future suddenly uncertain but they seem to take it all in their stride. I wonder how I would have reacted at their age.

My days are spent in the office, often packing beer and working out the latest advice on when tourism may be allowed to reopen. I get used to zoom calls, webinars and conference calls. Then I ride out over the hills and try not to think about the future too much.

We are encased in a bubble away from a world that has temporarily stopped turning and we can appreciate the environment around us.

Phase 3: June/July

ON the 18th June, Nicola Sturgeon announces her route out of lockdown. Now, there is a timetable and dates and the beginning of a path back to reality. Do we want to go back to reality – the old reality or a new reality? Could we do things differently here? Will the old models work or will we have to think of new ways to do business. Forecasting the future is frightening and exhausting to contemplate.

We embark on a series of mini home made videos to explore the history of the house and allow people to see inside while we are closed. We are working on plans to become more self sufficient in the café, develop a project with young people to grown our own fruit and veg; developing a mail order business for the brewery and we talk about developing the Traquair Historical Society.

We plan to open the café for takeaway and the grounds on the 17th July but there is suddenly a mountain of paperwork to deal with. Risk assessments, signage and ppe to order. I find some days I am yearning to get back to those days in April when we could not even contemplate re-opening.

Yet, we have to tiptoe out of this crisis and there is a sense of excitement along with some trepidation here. It will be good to see people around at Traquair once more, the sense of community here that sustains many of us and there will be a huge challenge ahead. We can only try to remain positive and hope the new horizon ahead will offer unforeseen benefits over the one we left behind.

PW: Catherine, Traquair looks to have been an excellent place to be to cope with a lockdown. Thank you for sharing, lovely picsxx

BD: Finally catching up on all your fascinating contributions, Decameroners, or should it be Decameronets? Either way, thank you for your thoughts, and Catherine, I share so much of your journey in motherhood. My first child was born when I was almost 39!!!

DJ: I was 38. A good age - I think!

BD: Dear Mark, such a powerful contribution and great memory for me of the Dining Room. But my little Traquair location keeps flooding back in my dreams. The Walled Garden on a sunny day. Bliss!

DJ: So well said Catherine. X

PW: Interesting contributions Mark, Andrew and Catherine. Lots to consider. Let's hope we do see some good come out of this difficult time, for me lockdown an extremely lonely time. People may have changed but not necessarily for the better. My brother told me he was at Tesco the other day and he thanked the girl who served him. She looked surprised and told him he was the first person to thank her that day some 6 hours after starting her shift. Not sure what to think about that.

Mark Muller Stuart

Postscript: Delilah

JUST after having posted my last and somewhat celebratory 10th Decameron – highlighting our idyll experience of Lockdown at Traquair - we awoke the next morning to discover that one of our number was likely going to depart from us. Delilah, our beloved King Charles Spaniel, as I reported in my last Decameron, was no longer eating or walking very much.

As the Vet smelt her breath and diagnosed regressive kidney failure, we knew time was short. The stench from her mouth was plague-like yet her loyal gaze as she looked up to us seem to embrace life itself.

We spent the weekend tending to her knowing that the Vet would come on Tuesday at 3pm to put her down. She had been placed on death's row and so had we as her executioners.

I was mortified as I have a very strong sense of protection towards my family. My mind sought out how we could rescue her or delay her passing in a pathetic attempt to trump life itself. Suddenly images and elements of trauma of the 19-year battle my family waged against my Mother's breast, ovarian, bone and brain cancer came back to the surface.

She had been told on five separate occasions over ten years that she had only a month to live only to go on and on. We had spent many of those days helping her to confront her own mortality. It's difficult to look at a loved one and know they are about to be taken. At least Delilah did not have to contemplate her own passing although there did seem an intensity to her gaze. Every moment I spent over the weekend with Delilah became almost visceral as she continued to look up towards me with total loyalty.

On Tuesday morning she duly followed her mistress to the office at Traquair as she had done each morning for the past 15 1/2 years. It was heart-breaking to watch her slowly walk back through the gates of the courtyard at Traquair for the last time as Catherine returned for lunch.

It was 1.30pm. As we gathered for the last lunch, I made some silly comment about how I was almost Buddhist in my dislike of killing things. My son retorted: 'Dad what are you taking about – Buddhists understand that death is part of the very circle of life.'

The comment made me sit up as he calmly told me how it was better for Delilah to go now without pain than suffer as her mother, Daphne, had done when her organs had failed her three years earlier. My daughter, Charlotte, then talked of how it was not a sad event at all as she was going to pass peacefully.

I began to feel somewhat ashamed at my over sentimentalised mournful state. Rather than rescue my children they had rescued me with a better, fresher perspective on life itself. I watched as they cuddled Delilah and said their respective goodbyes with grace and tenderness.

I then left for Edinburgh with Charlotte as Delilah spent her last few moments alone with Catherine on her lap in the old living room of Traquair. At 3pm, the Vet came to inject her. She fell quietly asleep for 30 minutes before the heart-stopping injection was applied.

Catherine said she did not suffer and when I later saw her in the second cellar in her box wrapped in a white shroud, she did indeed seem at peace. The next day she was buried next to her mother, Daphne, in the grounds of Traquair.

I remember riding past her and thinking about the cycle of life. I was struck by both a sense of grief but also of her passing as we moved away from the guillotine of time ticking away.

Yet this grief was nothing compared to what others must have suffered during Lockdown when their loved ones were suddenly taken away from them by Covid.

Many of them weren't even allowed to be with their loved ones or be allowed to mourn their passing. I rode on feeling blessed by the time we had been given over the weekend.

Three days later, Catherine's little guinea pig unaccountably also died. Suddenly the spirit of the 10th Decameron I recounted but just a few days ago, seemed an age away. We had truly come to the end of its cycle.

Traquair finally opened to the public two days after Delilah's death. Then Andrew reported to me that he was going to France with Michael for a holiday. As I write this I myself am now due to fly to Italy tomorrow but not before our final drinks tonight.

Lockdown has truly ended as we knew it and life has begun its remorseless march once again. It was almost poetic of Delilah to remind us of life's full cycle on the 100th day of Decameron.

It gave an extra meaning to the whole experience of it and that is why I decided to pen this postscript – so that we may also honour Delilah tonight – and through doing so – not only welcome her into the arms of the Decameronites of 2020 – but also record for posterity her spirit, life and times for she was as much a part of Decameron at Traquair than any of us.

CS: Wonderful Mark - your best yet. I identify with so much in your words both personal and political.

Louis and Delilah, 2020.